DIFFERENT, BUT NO LESS

By the same author

The Best Thing about You Is YOU!

Lessons Life Taught Me, Unknowingly: An Autobiography

Your Best Day Is Today!

DIFFERENT, BUT NO LESS

The Unscripted Story behind the Making of ***Tanvi the Great***

ANUPAM KHER

HAY HOUSE

HAY HOUSE INDIA
New Delhi • London • Sydney
Carlsbad, California • New York City

Hay House Publishers (India) Pvt Ltd
Muskaan Complex, Plot No. 3, B-2, Vasant Kunj, New Delhi – 110070, India

Hay House LLC, P.O. Box 5100, Carlsbad, CA 92018-5100, USA
Hay House UK Ltd, 1st Floor, Crawford Corner, 91-93 Baker Street, London W1U 6QQ, UK
Hay House Australia Publishing Pty Ltd, 18/36 Ralph St., Alexandria NSW 2015, Australia

Email: contact@hayhouse.co.in
Website: www.hayhouse.co.in

First published by Hay House India, 2025
10 9 8 7 6 5 4 3 2 1

ISBN 978-93-6611-180-3 (Hardback)
ISBN 978-93-6611-992-2 (Ebook)

Printed at Thomson Press

MIX
Paper | Supporting responsible forestry
FSC® C010615
FSC www.fsc.org

Hay House is committed to a sustainable future for our business, our readers and our planet. This book is made from Forest Stewardship Council® certified paper.

This book is dedicated to the Indian Armed Forces for their courage, sacrifice, and unwavering spirit.

To extraordinary souls like Tanvi, who remind us that being different is a kind of brilliance.

And to all those who never give up. May your strength continue to light the way for others.

Contents

Foreword

by Mahesh Bhatt

TRUTH WALKED INTO THE VILLAGE, NAKED AND UNINVITED. It stood there—raw, unfiltered, without apology. The naked truth is a terrifying thing. It doesn't soften the blow. It doesn't comfort, doesn't entertain. It just stands there, unrelenting. And so, the doors slammed. Curtains were drawn. People turned away.

Truth, battered and bewildered, wandered into the wilderness, asking itself, 'What use am I if no one will look at me?' That is when Story found it.

Story was the magician, the charmer, the eternal seducer. It had walked through time, slipping Truth into fables, wrapping it in myths, and lacing it with music. 'They will never take you as you are,' Story whispered. 'But let me dress you up, and they will listen.' And so, Truth allowed itself to be clothed.

Wrapped in metaphor, painted with colour, adorned with rhythm, Truth returned to the village. This time, they let it in. They welcomed it and even called it wisdom. But was it really Truth they had embraced or just the disguise that made it easier to swallow?

This is how it has always been. This is why Buddha spoke in riddles, why Jesus told parables, why Rumi hid revelations in poetry. And this is why the Ramayana and the Mahabharata still hold us captive. They are not just epics; they are living, breathing testimonies to the power of Story—stories so potent, so deeply embedded in our bones, that they continue to shape us long after their words were first spoken.

The important point here is that Truth alone is unbearable, but Truth wrapped in a Story can move mountains. And that is exactly what Anupam Kher has done. He has taken a truth so raw, so brutal in its beauty, and given it the wings of a Story. He calls it *Tanvi the Great*. It is the tale of an autistic girl who is not broken, not lacking . . . just different. A girl who sees the world through a lens most of us are too blind to understand. Through this daringly original film, drawn from his own lived experience, Anupam becomes a powerful voice for autism.

'Autism is not a disability, it is a different ability,' as a prominent figure in the autism community reminds us. Tanvi's story, beautifully portrayed by Anupam, exemplifies this truth. It is a testament to the fact that every child with autism is unique, and every child deserves to be understood.

When Anupam first shared this story with me, it shook me. In an age when cinema has become so cautious, so eager to please, he has dared to rebel. He has dared to tell a story that does not ask for permission.

So, *Tanvi the Great* will play. The lights will dim, the music will rise, and for a while, you will forget yourself. And when the film ends, when the credits roll and the lights come back on, something will stay with you. A whisper. A pulse. A truth you cannot unsee.

'Autism is not a roadblock, it is a detour,' as someone with lived experience of autism beautifully puts it. Tanvi's story, through Anupam's masterful storytelling, will guide us on that detour—a journey of understanding, acceptance, and celebration of the unique tapestry of human existence. But before that, warm yourself by reading the book—the tale of how this truth fought to be born, the hands that tried to strangle it, the battle that had to be waged so it could breathe.

You will like the book. But I swear to you that you will love the film, and you will never be the same again!

1

Putting the Cart Before the Horse

'A BOOK ABOUT A FILM THAT IS YET TO BE RELEASED?' I believe the last time my publisher looked this bewildered must have been when he saw a complex algebra problem as a compulsory twenty-mark question in his board exams! And I understood his dilemma. Yes, there are hundreds of books on which films have been made, or books that have been written to encash the success of films that became benchmarks of cinema. But this book does not fall into any such category. And for those who are still trying to guess, it is not even akin to Eric Segal's *Love Story,* because it is not a screenplay-turned-into-novel of my upcoming film.

Of course, now that you have started reading it, you will soon discover the interesting story that inspired me to wear the director's hat once again after a long gap of twenty-two years for my upcoming film, *Tanvi the Great.* But what this book is all about is something else. First, let me share what inspired me to be an author again.

Our film's protagonist, Tanvi Raina, is a young girl whose stream of thoughts is as pure as one that has just flowed from a glacier—pristine, uncontaminated, and transparent. We envisioned and created a world marked between the longitudes and latitudes of goodness and innocence for *Tanvi the Great*. In order to do that in the most credible way, it was imperative for me to discover, feel, and believe in the goodness around me. Staying in touch with innocence became a prerequisite, much like providing your Aadhaar card number before filling out any form in India. And the challenge is that innocence is a one-time-usage virtue; it is like an OTP of virtues. Once you have lost it, it is gone forever. You can't get it back. Moreover, losing the ability to be innocent is a one-way street, and sadly, the world around us often pushes us to walk down that road.

While working on this film, however, I had to stay in touch with innocence and goodness. For honest storytelling, I had to see only the beautiful side of life and the people around me. Just like our protagonist, Tanvi Raina, tells her grandpa, 'Mumma says always look at the beautiful side.' I had to spot positivity even in the most trying and disheartening situations—something that gave me a new perspective and empowered me with a new vision. To put it in a more contemporary articulation, the making of this film enriched me with great life lessons.

Yet, despite these enriching lessons, the journey was far from easy. As if the intrinsic challenges that come embedded with the process of filmmaking were not enough, I had to face numerous external and additional challenges too. The hardships were not just creative; they were also financial, mental, and of course, physical—all rolled in together! While I was not making a typical masala movie, making this movie had all the masala of—ironically—a commercial entertainer! However, the bitter truth about filmmaking is that, at the end of the day, it is an art form tied to commerce. Even the so-called 'arthouse' films carry a commercial angle, simply because money goes into making them. So, whether a film wears the 'commercial' tag or not, there is always a commercial side to it.

I was the captain of the ship with some two hundred and fifty people on board. Even before we could sail out of the docks, there was a storm ahead. Just a few days prior to the shoot, when everything and everyone was poised to travel with me to the quaint shooting location of Lansdowne—a small army town in the picturesque state of Uttarakhand in north India—I got the jolt of my life! The tracks on which my dream train was all set to run had some loose nuts, and so an indefinite delay, if not derailment, looked close to inevitable. By all permutations and combinations of logical reasoning, it seemed wiser to abandon the voyage than to go ahead into troubled waters. That is what my mind was quietly telling me, while Herman D'Souza, CEO of Anupam Kher Studios, was saying it out loud. But . . .

'But' is arguably the most interesting word in our vocabulary. It has the power to change fortunes. Depending on its placement, it can either mark the end or a new beginning.

So yes, things did look significantly discouraging. But then I reminded myself that I am an actor, not a regular filmmaker. I cannot spell passion as p-r-o-j-e-c-t. Such speed breakers cannot become roadblocks on my journey. I have been chosen as the medium to tell this inspiring story to the world. It is a responsibility I am meant to shoulder. And so, it was time for the superhero to emerge out of Clark Kent. I gathered all the courage I could and moved ahead.

However, before actually believing that I was Mr Kent, I had a few questions to answer. How will I beat the odds? Under these challenging circumstances, how will I maintain the much-needed calmness essential for taking the right creative calls? How am I supposed to differentiate between fortitude and indulgence? My acting assignments could make most of my colleagues green with envy, so why on earth would I switch gears and put myself in such a tough spot? Had I suddenly developed an appetite for extreme sports, like skydiving without a parachute?

The answers to these questions actually taught me some great lessons. They empowered me with a sense of achievement and courage. They made me richer by the soul—a nice phrase to use when you are poorer by the bank balance—to such an extent that I felt it was imperative to share these learnings with everyone. I also, somehow, have always seen my life like an autobiography. All the wisdom I gathered during the making of *Tanvi the Great* has added a few more important chapters to the book of my life, and I believe they are worth a read.

This book is not about storms. It is about sailing through them. It is about not letting anyone else get affected by your own predicament. It is about putting your faith in your own self to the test. It is about optimism and hope. It is about finding your way through the chaos. It is about following the greatest GPS God has gifted us—our heart.

So, if the intent of this book is to share whatever I gathered, then why wait for the film to release? In other words, why wait to share something good? Therefore, it didn't matter whether the film had been released or not. This book is meant to help all of us. It is not an epilogue to the film or my life. Instead, its purpose is to restore your faith in goodness and innocence. It is meant to inspire an MBA and a budding filmmaker alike. It is about getting signals of hope in the SIM card of your heart, even in a bad network area! And that is what I explained to my publisher. And now, you are holding this copy in your hands or on your screen.

Happy reading!

2

Life Likes Surprises and Loves the Stubborn

January is the month for the unboxing of the New Year. Everyone, with renewed excitement, is in the mood to make resolutions, ranging from the most mundane to the most monumental ones. I had already made mine more than a year back, and now I was all set to live up to it in the year 2024. This is why, to me, this New Year looked newer than any of the New Years I had welcomed in the last two decades, at least. Of course, I had a great reason to be partial towards this New Year—because the shooting of my dream, *Tanvi the Great*, was about to commence in the next month! 2024 was indeed a leap year for me, in more ways than one.

I returned from Delhi on New Year's Eve with the script draft file saved as 'TTG-Final-Final' on my iPad. And that file name pretty much said it all! Once in Mumbai, I was in marathon meetings with my direction team associates and other department heads, while typing or recording some three to four thousand 'Same to you' New Year messages on the side.

There was more exuberance than blood in my veins. Prep work was going on with the greatest possible intensity. I wanted everything to be well-planned and well-managed so that everyone had the best and most memorable experience while making this film. After all, we were creating the blissful, utopian world of Tanvi. So, the real life ought to match the reel life somewhere.

A few days later, we had made our travel agent busy too. We were ready with a long list of about 250 names. These were the names of the crew members—across departments—who were going to travel with us to Lansdowne, a small town in the state of Uttarakhand, at a height of 1,780 metres above sea level. Being the headquarters of the valiant Garhwal Rifles, the administration of this little-more-than-a-century-old town is also looked after by the Cantonment Board. Therefore, we prepared ID cards for each and every member of the crew.

One afternoon, Pranit Kher, the director's assistant on this film and coincidentally my nephew, walked in with the samples of ID cards printed for the crew members. The designs looked really nice and elegant, and he wanted my approval.

'Hotels have been booked,' he informed further. 'We now only need to make a list of who is staying where—the room allocation, basically.'

I nodded, smiled, and gave a go-ahead look. This somewhat measured response from me betrayed the enthusiasm I had been wearing on my sleeve by that point. I don't think Pranit noticed it; only I knew the reason for this.

I had been trying to reach out to the gentleman who had agreed to come on board as our chief financier and co-producer of the film. For the last few weeks, for reasons best known to him, he was being evasive—or so I felt. A lot of my calls were not being answered promptly, and the replies to my messages were also getting terser by the day. And yes, we did exchange the mandatory, saccharine-sweet New Year wishes a few days back, but now was the time to discuss something far more urgent—the transfer of funds. I had been following up with him, reminding him about our agreement for a few months. I could sense that things were moving at a pace slower than expected. And one expected a lot more curiosity, involvement, and participation from someone who had expressed great interest and passion in the story. I assumed that being a busy and successful businessman, he must be really hard-pressed for time. But now it was our turn to be hard-pressed for time.

We were travelling to a location where no film crew had ever shot anything before. We were going to be the first ones to shoot a full-fledged movie there. We, as producers of the film, were responsible for the safety and comfort of these 250 people who had come together to make a dream come true.

In the midst of all this logistical madness and excitement, I was still chasing down our main financier, hoping everything would come together soon. Finally, after much relentless persuasion on my part, our chief financier responded, and he refused to transfer the money at that juncture—just 25 days away from the shoot. Yes, he had pulled out of the project!

Think about my plight as the producer-director! Two hundred and fifty people were waiting for the shoot to begin, and dozens of invoices from technicians were piling up in the inbox of Herman D'Souza. Meanwhile, I sat in my cabin, staring blankly at a map of Lansdowne on my laptop screen. To me, the height of Lansdowne looked way higher than 1,780 metres above sea level, as mentioned on the screen.

We had everything and everyone geared up for the shoot, except the money and the co-producer, who now said that his board of directors did not agree to spare funds as they were hesitant to invest money in a film venture. He sounded like a scratch card saying, 'Better luck next time.' The journey to make *Tanvi the Great* had become an uphill one indeed.

Suddenly, I noticed something I had scribbled long ago on a piece of paper on my desk. I pushed it to Herman. He read it: 'Life likes surprises. But it loves the stubborn.' If his silence didn't, the look on Herman's face said it aloud—this was the time for action, not philosophical reflection! After that pregnant pause, he suggested we postpone the shoot. Much to my disappointment, I had to bury the moment loaded with great cinematic poignancy and explain to him what I had on my mind.

After being on the roller coaster of life for more than six decades, I knew that throwing surprises was life's favourite pastime. It really likes to do so with everyone—only the frequency and intensity vary. But what it truly loves is the stubbornness of those who do not give up easily. After all, like all of us, life too doesn't enjoy one-sided matches. It exults when someone is ready to give good competition as a worthy opponent, even with their back to the wall! And hence, I decided to pull out my old pair of boxing gloves—metaphorically, of course.

I felt as if Tanvi was waiting for us in Lansdowne, ready to join us, and if we didn't go now, she would be left there, waiting for us forever. I couldn't shake the feeling that we might lose her and never see her again. There was no way I could have thought of doing that to her. A voice within me whispered that if this film does not get made now, it won't get made ever, and that was also not acceptable. Along with me, a lot of other people had invested their time and energies into this project by now. Being an artist myself, I felt a deep sense of responsibility towards them. I had to find a way out. It was time to fight back because life loves the stubborn!

3

A Full Vessel Cannot Hold New Raindrops

It is good to gather knowledge from every experience of life and have a sense of fulfilment. But I believe this sense of fulfilment must be juxtaposed with a sense of emptiness. A vessel that is filled to the brim cannot hold even a drop more. There should always be some empty space to gather the fresh raindrops.

However, we were lucky it wasn't raining that day. It was the year 2021, and I was attending the wedding of my niece (my brother Raju Kher's daughter), Vrinda, in Delhi. It was a cold, slightly foggy afternoon. I even precisely remember the time: 12:37 p.m. Everyone was singing, dancing, or mirthfully chatting around the bride-to-be.

As already mentioned, I always look at my life like an autobiography in the making and that is why I have this habit of preserving moments of my life on camera every day. Thus, I was busy capturing the spirit of the 'great Indian wedding' at a Delhi farmhouse—an epithet that would help many to imagine the visual with greater accuracy.

As my camera panned left, towards the edge of the lawns, I noticed that the teenage daughter of my first cousin, Priyanka, was standing away from everyone and staring at the verdant surroundings around the farmhouse. I walked up to her and asked what she was looking at. She replied without shifting her gaze, 'I am looking at my world.' It was a seemingly simple but deeply profound answer. The depth and dimensions of this young girl's articulation seeped into my soul immediately.

This girl was Tanvi Anand—my niece. And in that moment, she gifted me the idea of making a movie that would be destined to be as close to my heart as a child is to its mother. On that day, in that moment, I heard a voice within telling me that I would make a film about Tanvi's world . . . a film titled *Tanvi the Great*.

I grew up in a close-knit family with Indian middle-class values, where the term 'cousin' was rarely used. We were all, by and large, brothers and sisters. If someone, for some reason, got extra curious—like the census folks who want to know every detail of the family—we would use expressions like *mamere, mausere, chachere, bhai,* and *behen* to explain our relationship instead of calling each other cousins. Maternal or paternal cousins are like the pre-installed apps of friendship in our lives.

So, our sister Priyanka, whom we all address as Deepu, is married to an Indian Army officer posted in Tezpur, Assam. Deepu's father, Shri P. L. Kher (my father's younger brother, lived with us for many years, and hence our bond had welded us really close.

Being Deepu's daughter, Tanvi was very special to all of us. And being an autistic child, she held a unique place in the world as well. I had met Tanvi on a number of occasions earlier as well, and each time, I would be taken aback by her innocence and purity.

It is my belief that while all of us are born innocent, the world contaminates our innocence sooner or later. Fortunately, this is not the case with people like Tanvi. Their purity is flawless and world-proof. That is why Tanvi's statement touched the chord of my soul with great intensity. Now I wanted to see her world through my eyes. I felt this world of goodness and purity must be explored and shown to everyone—to remind us how the Almighty wanted us to be! It was the need of the hour. Tanvi suddenly gave me a new purpose, a new milestone to cross in my journey as an artist and as a storyteller!

I wonder what would have happened if I had not paid attention to what she said. What if I had kept my receptive mode off? Her statement would have brushed past me like a whiff of air. That moment and that answer proved that we must always be like a vessel with a little emptiness—a bit of space to absorb and accommodate something new. That is the only way to gather new ideas and experiences in life. If we want new ideas to seep into us, we have to be in a receptive mode, like a vessel with a little emptiness and not filled to the brim. You never know when the raindrops of a fresh idea may come in!

4

More Nourishment Only Makes an Idea Better

The idea planted in my mind after that fateful meeting with Tanvi soon began to take root in my heart. I wanted it to blossom into a full-fledged film. And for sure, it did not look like a distant or impossible dream to me. After all, I have read enough self-help books to know that if you can dream it, you can do it! Eventually, it became difficult to decipher whether the idea was consuming me more or whether it was the other way around.

This process of mutual consumption was further accentuated by the fact that in my professional life, I had never, ever turned the take-a-break mode on. Right from the day I put on my acting shoes—actually, the whitener for *Saaransh*—I have been running a never-ending but soul-satiating marathon. In fact, after *Saaransh* and *Karma,* I found myself so caught up in work that I barely had time to notice life or the world around me. It was all about rushing from one studio to another. While I loved the work, I was always in fast-forward mode. To balance this pace, I started spending time with children at Dilkhush Special School in Juhu, Mumbai. (In the early to mid-1990s, I taught, conducted workshops, and engaged with students at Dilkhush Special School—a dedicated institution for children with special needs.)

The idea for a film about someone like Tanvi came during what I consider the most creatively fulfilling phase of my career. My time in the US, working with incredible actors like my friend Bob (Robert De Niro) and others, really sharpened me as an actor and taught me how to achieve more by doing less. This was a phase where I was enjoying the craft, working with fresh talent, experimenting, and most importantly, soaking in whatever life threw my way every day. But suddenly, like a newborn, this story began demanding all my attention and time. The urge to immerse myself in it grew stronger and more compelling by the day.

Fortunately, I was scheduled to go to Kerala for a rejuvenation session at a health resort for a few days. It was a quaint and quiet place where you could hear the chirping of birds as much as you could hear your own heartbeat. (Mine was pumping more than just blood to my veins!) The trained therapists at that health resort were very happy to see me getting energetic, cheerful, and recharged in consistent progression, every day. They were beaming because I was beaming. Palpably, they must have assumed that their efforts—along with their forty-two-odd yogic ways of push and pulls, twists and turns—were working well on their celebrity client. That could have been true also—after all, they had charged me a bomb for those twists and turns—but I believe the idea I had been nurturing was nourishing me all the time.

Finally, it was time to pass on the infection of excitement to someone else. So, I told the story idea to my true friend and a great pillar of strength, Herman, who was also soaking in the calm, detoxifying environment of that health resort with me. By talking to him about the possibility of making a film on a girl like Tanvi, I bestowed upon Herman the title of the first person with whom the idea of this film was shared. A privileged status indeed!

Herman is the runway from which my dreams take off. And being in charge of the commercial aspect of my profession, he is judicious in spending both—the currency in the bank and the currency of words. He spends both in accurately measured proportions and only when necessary. Herman loved the idea, and his positive response was the first shot of encouragement I got.

Our stay at that rejuvenation resort was over soon. I thanked the staff there but did not tell them that the thought of making a film was far more rejuvenating and therapeutic than all of their therapies put together.

Once back in Mumbai, my routine resumed, albeit with a new dimension added to it—the burning desire and determination to bring the story of Tanvi to life. This happens because the ideas you truly believe in have a way of pulling your attention and love automatically. The only question was, how do I create some space to work on the idea?

Do you remember how we used to hide comic books inside our schoolbooks—I am making a safe assumption that almost all of us have done this as children—and read them? That is exactly what was happening with me! For the world, I may have been taking a shower, but in reality, I was soaking my mind in the events that could make an interesting story. For the world, when I was relishing the peanut *chikki* (peanut brittle or candy) I am super possessive about, I was actually chewing upon the conflicts that may spring up in Tanvi's life. (Yes, by then I had made up my mind to name the protagonist of my film also Tanvi.) When I was running on the treadmill in the morning, I was thinking how far this story could go. While interacting with my students at Actor Prepares, I often found myself wondering if Tanvi was hiding within one of them. I would wake up in the middle of the night, and even in those hours of darkness, the thought of making this film would dazzle my consciousness.

Are you wondering why I am giving so many juxtapositions here? That is to explain what this story meant to me and in what proportions it had engulfed my existence! So obviously, any obstacle in the way was bound to hit me harder than anybody else. And that is the reason the pre-shooting turbulence hurt me deeply. However, my confidence was stirred but not shaken. We shall come back to obstacles later. Right now, at this stage, there was yet another important learning to be taken home.

As already mentioned by way of a wide variety of examples, my mind was working on the idea around the clock. One afternoon, on the way to the legendary Film City, I got stuck in what looked like one of the slowest possible traffic jams. I checked on Google Maps and it showed up an alternative route with the same ETA but with more kilometres. I told my driver, Sunil, to take that alternative route. He mumbled that with the map showing a similar ETA, it wouldn't make much of a difference. Since there was ample time at hand, I thought of succinctly explaining to him the perspective he was missing: if we cover more kilometres in the same time, it means the traffic on the longer route is lesser than the shorter one, and so at least driving can be a bit easier.

Sunil heard me but did not react for a few seconds and then started nodding his head. Though we were nowhere close to any peepal tree, Sunil looked at me with his eyes gleaming as if he had just had a moment of epiphany while sitting under one. He mumbled something to the effect of thanking me for enlightening him about the possibility of a different perspective; he used the word *nazariyaa* to communicate 'perspective'.

I smiled and tried to re-enter the world of Tanvi in my head. But suddenly, I realised it was my turn to find a seat under a peepal tree! While I was working very hard as the creator of the imaginary world of Tanvi, I needed someone who could add more dimensions and perspectives to it. I needed to collaborate with some good writer/writers before moving to the next stage of screenplay writing.

I knew very well that while forming a team for yourself, you should know what kind of people you are most likely to be comfortable with. Different visions fetch different perspectives, but too much of a difference can result in abrasive friction. So, a leader needs to have the ability to find the right balance. Therefore, I wanted to look for writers who were sensitive and empathetic. They had to love the subject as much as I did and see the world of possibilities in it.

Over the years, I have learnt that a good story can only flow from a good heart. I did not want the tricks or the academic formula of screenplay writing to overshadow the natural flow of storytelling. This story needed people who could see the world of Tanvi through her eyes. I was quite clear that I didn't want to team up with a writer who would try—or had previously tried—to impress 'Anupam Kher' with their script narrations. I wanted very unpretentious people around me. After all, writing a script together and then taking it to the stage of execution meant a lot of time would be spent with these people. So, it was important for them to be good-hearted and real.

Now, if you are wondering what kind of scanner could possibly help to find a person like that, let me share a little secret: I have been blessed with the ability to see through the people around me. There is some kind of a CT scan planted in me that shows me the true nature of the people I deal with—not always, but usually. Thankfully, the search for the writers was short-lived because I found them soon.

Ankur Suman was both my best friend and the writer for the late Satish Kaushik. He had written *Kaagaz 2*, which was Satish's last production. I was playing a pivotal role in this film on a sensitive, emotional subject. The scenes and dialogues were written with maturity and depth. During our interactions and discussions, I found Ankur took feedback positively and had the ability to come up with good solutions quickly—perhaps a skill he had acquired while working in the advertising world for years.

While we were shooting some patchwork for *Kaagaz 2*, I shared the concept and a video clip of Tanvi with Ankur in the vanity van. He loved the idea and immediately saw great potential in it. But since he was already working with Satish on a couple of other projects, he said he would have to seek permission to come on board, which I knew he wouldn't get. After all, Satish was my best friend. I knew he was passionate about his films and possessive about his team members. I also admired Ankur's sense of loyalty because he could have immediately said yes to me, instead of asking Satish. Moreover, one of Satish's projects was about to go on the floors, and hence, I could not poach his favourite writer. Thus, my search for the right writer continued.

Soon, my quest led me to my friend, Sooraj Barjatya, one of India's top producers and directors. His family's banner, Rajshri Films, as every Indian cinema lover would agree, is known for creating clean, heartfelt films with sincere intent and a deep understanding of human emotions. I told Sooraj I was looking for a writer who could craft a beautiful, emotionally rich journey that moved at its own pace, not just a well-structured, three-act screenplay. That is when Sooraj reminded me of the writer of *Uunchai*—my latest Rajshri film with Sooraj as the director. *Uunchai* was about a journey of self-discovery and had been written in a very gentle, mature, yet entertaining way. Sooraj recommended its writer, Abhishek Dixit, who had also been nominated for the Filmfare Award for best dialogues for the film.

I asked Sooraj since he knew me and my requirements, why he thought Abhishek fit the bill. Sooraj replied, 'Because apart from being a good writer, Abhishek is a good listener too.' I did not feel the need to question Sooraj's recommendation any further after this.

I met Abhishek and he was on board as soon as I applied the last full stop to my narration. He asked for a few days' time and returned soon with a very emotional and inspiring story of Tanvi's journey. Now it was my turn to sign him up as soon as he applied the last full stop to his narration. I had tears of joy in my eyes and some cash (as a token of the signing amount) in my hand. Abhishek Dixit was on board!

Just as we began our journey, tragedy struck. Satish passed away, and the projects he was working on along with Ankur obviously came to a halt. Ankur met me, and I felt his background in advertising could bring a fresh perspective to the story. After our meeting, he made his decision quickly, turning down a project he was about to start and choosing to join us instead. And with this, I had my writing team in place!

It would have been very easy to give in to the temptation of developing the subject alone, but then even the best of batsmen needs a bowler to improve his game. One needs to have the ability to trust others and make room for newer ideas and suggestions. Remember, more nourishment only makes your idea stronger and sharper. So, pick your team carefully, thoughtfully, and once done, trust them.

5

To Know What You Want, First Know What You Don't

NOW, WITH BOTH WRITERS ON BOARD AND FILES TITLED *Tanvi the Great—Draft 1* and *Tanvi the Great—Draft 2* on my iPad, things were finally starting to look promising. Ideas were making their way like a stream of water flowing down hills, clearing the path on their own. And the best part was that it was like a stream during the monsoon—not just free-flowing but overflowing. It felt as if we had been issued visas to step into Tanvi Raina's world—one that was finally coming to life for real! But even as the groundwork was laid and our creative energy soared, the practical realities of filmmaking loomed over us.

Confidence is the greatest currency that can truly enrich your life. However, the world has yet to officially accept it as a currency, which means, to make a film, one still needs the official currency. This meant it was time to find like-minded producers for this film—people who could see as much potential in Tanvi's world as I did.

At the time, Jyoti Deshpande was producing several films for Jio, Reliance's relatively new OTT platform, and there was a lot of promising buzz in the industry around her initiatives. I am not sure whose bad luck it was, but when I tried reaching out, she couldn't take my calls. Those were early days, and she was likely swamped at the time. Still, I wasn't discouraged. I told myself that with such a fresh and unique subject, I wouldn't be short of options. With that faith, I met a couple of top-notch producers—the truly A++ level, blue-blooded ones. Both of them were very happy to know that I had decided to direct after a long gap of twenty-two years. They were quite encouraging and helpful too. In fact, they were so helpful that one of them chatted with me at length about the kind of songs we must have in the film, going by the contemporary music taste of the audience. I have a feeling that if the meeting had lasted even ten minutes longer, he might have suggested adding a party song or maybe even a bhangra number to make the film more saleable. As I mentioned earlier, my invisible mind-reading super-chip kicked in, and I could already sense where the meeting was headed. So, I politely excused myself.

The other producer was also extremely forthcoming and extended his help by way of casting suggestions. He recommended the name of a young actress who has been around for a while. I did not disagree with him. I just told him that I would prefer to make this film on my own. I did so because it would have been impossible for him to understand why this film required a fresh face. The fact is that when you are going to jump off a plane for skydiving, you should not have people around you cautioning you about risks that are part and parcel of the dive! Else, you would never be able to dive.

A few more discussions with colleagues, well-wishers, and friends from the industry convinced me that if I needed to swim against the tide, I must make my own arms stronger. I could have agreed with any of the producers and immediately got a green signal, along with the green bag full of signed papers and good money to make the film. But my objective was not to make just another film. My mission was to show the world that there was still some hope for a world free of manipulations, deceit, and lies. I had grown up watching the good old cinema—the cinema of innocence—and that was what I wanted to bring back to the screen with this film. How could I do that with compromised beliefs!? Hence, it was important to convince the new generation that it was never too old-fashioned to be innocent. And that could be done only when I told this story the way I wanted to tell it—with absolute honesty and sincerity of purpose. So, when my friend Mr Ramesh Taurani of Tips Industries said that I should cut a deal with an OTT platform first, I had to shake my head because that would have meant parting with my absolute freedom. The reality is that an OTT platform, with all its marketing pressures and commercial demands, would have forced me into decisions I didn't want to make. My generation doesn't just click 'I Agree' on long lists of terms and conditions without thinking. I knew I had to step away from that situation.

I was in my twenties when I played the forthright, more dogmatic, and less pragmatic B. V. Pradhan in *Saaransh*. Somewhere, back then, I could feel the fragrance of my grandfather, Pandit Amarnath Kher, in that character. Back then, I had thought that when I grew as old as the character I was playing, I would imbibe some of his qualities in me. And today, at seventy, I won't be surprised if Pradhan's and my biometrics match because I can feel his presence within me. I wish to stand for my beliefs and values. That is how I have been in both my personal as well as professional life. Perhaps it was this remnant piece of Pradhan that did not allow me to give in so easily.

To tempt a creative mind that is holding an idea is not a tough thing to do in our industry. It might actually be easier than tempting a kid with candy! Because once you believe you have a good idea, you become desperate to see it brought to life. But that forthright and righteous Pradhan *saab* (sir) breathing within me whispered to me: 'It is okay even if you are not very clear about what to do, but you must most certainly be clear about what you do not wish to do!' So, we hit the dead end sooner than one expected but nevertheless, the experience was quite helpful.

Cut to my office in Model Town, near Kokilaben Hospital in Andheri, Mumbai. Herman and I were sitting across the table, making a list of the people who may like to turn superheroes for us—and producers for the world—by investing money in the film's production. (Grammatically, I could have used the word 'project', but I have personally struck off that word from all the dictionaries in my office and at home.)

I would be lying if I said the financial crunch didn't bother me. It wasn't a great place to be in. After spending decades in this industry, proving my talent not just across India but even in Hollywood, it stung that people didn't share my faith in my story, in my vision.

It would have been far simpler to just let it go and continue living peacefully as an actor. But being stubbornly passionate in your late sixties is no walk in the park—I had come to realise that. Then again, playing a convincing man in his sixties when you are actually in your twenties isn't exactly a cakewalk either! If I pulled that off once, I told myself, I could pull this off too. And eventually, through persistent efforts, we secured a meeting with an industrialist who had an impressive track record across multiple sectors, including shipping.

In our industry, the common saying is: '*Collaboration ke liye kundali se zyada enthusiasm match hona chahiye*' (For a collaboration to work, matching enthusiasm matters more than matching horoscopes). And here we were! We had found someone who seemed to believe in our idea, our dream, and agreed to come on board with the much-needed funds. A decent amount of money was pledged, and I had never felt richer. What I felt can be best expressed in Hindi, so pardon the detour: *Aaj mere paas original script idea bhi tha, direct karne ka iraada bhi, aur uske liye jeb mein paisa bhi!* (Today, I had an original script idea, the intent to direct it, and the money in my pocket to make it happen!) Now I could say 'no' to certain acting assignments and plan for a proper, dedicated writing session with my writers for a few days. I wished to be cut off from the world and work in a relaxed and creatively stimulating environment. And so, it was time for a writers' retreat!

Instead of opting for an island in Thailand, I chose the island nation of Sri Lanka. Seeing their visas in their respective mailboxes, my writers displayed greater interest in the film and took some extra shots of commitment that night. But then, our hosts in Sri Lanka decided to outshine my writers in terms of enthusiasm and sent me an itinerary that could easily serve as the official guide for anyone visiting the island nation. I did not want to break my imaginary 'I-shall-never-travel-only-for-vacation' oath. Of course, I would love to explore Sri Lanka someday, but this was supposed to be a writing camp where we wanted to see more of Tanvi's world than the beauty of Lankan beaches. I quickly realised this trip was veering dangerously close to being pro-tourism and anti-writing. I had to find an alternative with a better ROI! No prizes for guessing—if not Sri Lanka, where did we go? Yes, Goa is the right answer!

Before leaving for Goa with Abhishek and Ankur, I went to seek the blessings of my mentor, Mr Mahesh Bhatt. We had the contours of the story in place by then, and I narrated the same to him. His wrinkles metamorphosed into laugh lines, and his eyes sparkled. He was moved by the storyline. I could sense an organic spike in his already high-energy levels. He looked at me with the same admiration with which he had seen me back in the 80s during the *Saaransh* days! He even gave us a very valuable tip for the film's climax, in his signature style—sentences sprinkled with striking metaphors and sharp similes.

With his blessings in my heart and the assurance of money arriving for the payment of this ten-day-long writing camp in a nice five-star property in Goa, we took the flight of fantasy (a Vistara flight, actually).

As soon as we arrived in Goa, the writing sessions kicked off, and with each passing day, my confidence solidified into conviction. It took a couple of sessions for us to find our rhythm, but soon, ideas began to flow just like the rain outside. There was a quiet thrill in knowing we were building a world that had never been seen before. It was also during these days in Goa that I reaffirmed that the name of the film would be *Tanvi the Great*.

I was joined by my friend and physiotherapist, Ashish Kaushik, in Goa. Not because I am a fitness freak and love to move around with my entourage, but because of my fractured shoulder. If you are curious about my injury, all I can say is that the story behind it has its own share of heroism and inspiring determination. But let's save that for another time.

One day, we narrated the story to Ashish, and he loved it so much that he requested to barter my physio sessions for our writing sessions. He started participating in the writing sessions with full involvement. During the last few days of our writing camp, my brother Raju Kher and my sister-in-law also arrived. They too loved the story we had developed by then. These people are direct when it comes to critically evaluating scripts and ideas. That is why their words of appreciation only strengthened my belief in the story and my vision for it, and I felt certain that there was absolutely no need to budge under any kind of pressure.

A couple of months later, we had another writing session in Goa, where a renowned scriptwriting teacher graciously joined us to help us understand the nuances of screenwriting. He dedicated a lot of time to us, immersing himself in the story with complete devotion. We had a wonderful time, and we gained valuable insights. While the session provided fresh perspectives, it also gave us greater clarity and confidence about what we didn't need to do. I also realised that a story like ours doesn't fit neatly into traditional screenwriting frameworks, simply because it has no reference point. And that singularity had to be preserved throughout. That is why, before I decided what I wanted to do, I knew what I certainly didn't want to do!

6

Break the Assembly Line

In the Indian film industry, it is standard procedure to make space for songs while writing a script. By the time we are sure about the number and placement of songs, we have a clear understanding of the characters and their journeys. This typically gives the music composer a well-defined path to follow. However, one word that I had barred from entering my mind was 'conventional'.

Passion and process are not the best of friends. If you are passionate, you are bound to break the processes or care about them less. And if you believe in following the processes to the hilt and keeping them above everything else, then somewhere, at some point, passion is going to slip away from you like a dissatisfied, disappointed partner. I am not saying that the two cannot converge, or that those who follow one are superior to the others; it is just that in the field of art—or even in other areas—passion often plays the role of the ignition key that turns everything on. So, the idea was to let the world of Tanvi Raina blossom on its own, organically. It was like walking through an orchard, gathering only the fruits that had ripened naturally, rather than trying to hasten the harvest through artificial means.

Do you think I have lost my way and have been harping too much on this process-versus-passion debate without context? No, this is for a reason—I did not follow the established process of waiting for the script to shape up before working on the songs and music of the film.

I still don't have a clear answer to how or why, but even before the screenplay was written, I somehow knew exactly what kind of songs the story needed and where they would fit in to move it forward. And this was even before any music composer was signed!

We were working on the script at a beautifully designed cafe nestled within the hotel property in Goa when I was informed that Sri M. M. Keeravani sir—known to the world as M. M. Kreem—was available for a call. It was Neeraj who had helped arrange the call. Sri M. M. Keeravani was introduced to the Hindi film audience years ago by Bhatt saab (Mahesh Bhatt).

I stepped out of the cafe where we were working, called him, and narrated an abridged version of the storyline in about ten minutes. Ankur and Abhishek were looking at me curiously as I walked back to our 'writing desk'. It was not lunchtime yet, and we still had a lot of ground to cover on the screenplay that day, otherwise, I could have ordered a champagne. That was because the legendary, Oscar-winning music composer Keeravani sir had agreed to do my film! Ten minutes went into the story narration, and by the end of the remaining two, he was on board. (And this included the time spent on the customary hi and bye.)

Later, I got to know that Keeravani sir was on his way to a studio in Kochi for a TV show shoot when we first spoke about *Tanvi the Great.* So, it was definitely not a conducive environment for a director—returning to filmmaking after twenty years—to present an unfinished screenplay to an Oscar winner who was on his way to a TV show in a city he didn't even live in. And yet, he said 'yes' to me! Was the great composer too keen to team up with me? Or was I just plain lucky? I couldn't wrap my head around how this miracle had happened.

Keeravani sir's 'Tum Mile, Dil Khile' is one of my all-time favourite songs. Two of the directors I am close to—Bhatt saab and Neeraj Pandey—have worked with Keeravani sir, and the results have been fantastic. I knew I wanted someone like Keeravani sir, who could create music as different as Tanvi was from the ordinary. This was also the year Keeravani sir made India proud by bringing home the Oscar for 'Naatu Naatu' from his cousin Rajamouli's magnum opus, *RRR.* Since I wanted to make an international film, I thought it would be nice to have an Oscar winner support our endeavours.

A little more than a year later, when we were composing the background score with Keeravani sir—who by then had also become a great friend—I asked him what made him give his approval to the film in just a few minutes. His answer gave me goosebumps and moist eyes. The legendary maestro, who had worked with some of the best and most experienced names in Indian cinema, said that it was the clarity and brevity of my narration that convinced him of my ability as a director. He mentioned that there have been times when directors have taken three hours to narrate a two-hour film, but even in our short phone call, I came across as crystal clear to him, both in terms of the roadmap and the destination. That, he added, was a rare quality, something only a few of the great directors he had worked with ever displayed.

This was a valuable lesson for me, which is, that your content matters more than the condition of your presentation. To get a favourable outcome from a pitch, more than fancy slides, you need clarity of thought.

It is true that Keeravani saab's remuneration was at a level that made Herman question whether I was absolutely sure I wanted only him. However, this was when we had a commitment of investment from our partner in the shipping industry. So, the cost of bringing on a super-talented lyricist was not a concern. But we were caught off guard by an unexpected turn of events—the sudden exit of the super-talented lyricist we had roped in. Yes, I have deliberately kept the change of the lyricist subtle, mainly because it happened early on, before we had spent much time working together. How could I have known then that this was just a teaser of the storm waiting for me a few milestones ahead? We were still in the early stages of putting the music together, so no real harm was done, just a bit of extra effort to find that poetic soul who could truly do justice to the subject.

During this time, my mind, of all the plausible places, took me to the reception-cum-waiting area of Dr Agarwal's clinic, where a straightforward but loving elderly mother had once 'prescribed' me to work with her daughter. According to her, her daughter was a very talented writer-cum-lyricist. This elderly lady's husband had made a film with my wife, Kirron, a few years back, and that is how I knew the family including the daughter.

This affectionate lady was the mother of Kausar Munir, the celebrated lyricist of several successful and meaningful songs. I contacted Kausar, and she readily agreed to work on the songs at Keeravani saab's warm, homely studio. The whole experience was deeply soulful—almost divine—made even better by the incredibly delicious meals. (Fun fact: at Keeravani saab's studio, it is not just the melodies that are heavenly, the food is too!)

There was something important to learn here as well. While it was disappointing that the original lyricist stepped away from the project, I chose not to view it as a setback. Instead, I saw it as an opportunity to find the right creative match. And as it turned out, the result wasn't just better, it was the best thing I could have hoped for! In hindsight, having a woman with a higher emotional quotient and a deeper understanding of what it is like to write for a girl who struggles to express herself felt far more appropriate and powerful.

Soon enough, we were all in Hyderabad, where magic unfolded in a studio that felt as warm and inviting as home. To get a sense of the musical direction he had in mind, I requested Keeravani sir to start with Tanvi Raina's theme music. Then what he played for us was nothing short of pure magic. As I listened, I could suddenly see Tanvi walking through the mountains, gliding over clouds like a butterfly with wings of innocence. Music has the power to reveal what usually lies hidden, to make the invisible visible, and that is exactly what it did for me.

I did not have much experience of such musical *baithaks* (meetings or sessions), but once I got into them, I was like Anupam in Wonderland, amazed by the ability of the master to churn out magical melodies with so much ease! Then, of course, Kausar's words came in—obedient like kids in a classroom, but mischievous and cheerful like children in a playground. Emboldened and encouraged by Keeravani sir, I suggested that, just like the on-screen Tanvi, the playback singers should also be fresh voices or at least relatively unfamiliar to the audience. I thought such a combination would enhance the songs' impact on the audience. Keeravani sir loved, supported, and implemented the idea and got some really young, talented, relatively lesser-known talent for these songs.

Our sessions quickly became a beautiful collaboration, like two travellers lighting the path for each other with torches in hand. The clarity with which I envisioned Tanvi Raina inspired Keeravani saab to craft his lilting melodies.

And his music, in turn, helped me see her even more clearly with every note, with every tear. Tear? Did I say tear? Yes. Those tears were my silent applause—rising straight from the soul—as I listened to the genius at work.

Not only did the songs bring Tanvi Raina's world to life, but they also helped me understand and visualise her more vividly—her body language, favourite places, diction, and even her sense of humour. It happened only because Keeravani Saab had understood Tanvi so well. In fact, he once said something that stayed with me: it is the non-autistic mind that is truly abnormal because it is often clouded by strategies, agendas, lies, and manipulations. The autistic mind, on the other hand, is untouched by such impurities—perhaps exactly how God intended all of us to be. Also, after watching a very rough cut of the film, Keeravani Saab called up Bhatt saab and said that once this movie releases, a lot of parents will end up wishing they had a child like Tanvi!

The music sessions truly moved me deeply. It touched my soul and filled my eyes with tears and my heart with compassion. I cannot express the pride and gratitude I felt when Keeravani saab said that out of the 249 films he had worked on, *Tanvi the Great* would be among his top ten! He often said that working with me felt like enjoying a good dinner or going on a vacation—it never felt like work. But I believe the real magic came from him. When such beautiful compositions are being created, life truly feels like a holiday you never want to come back from! And it is not just his work; so much of the ease and joy he brings comes from who he is. To me, his very presence feels like an easy, hummable melody. I was truly grateful to God for sending the right financial support at the right moment. It allowed me to collaborate with Keeravani saab, who, with each passing day, was nurturing the soul of *Tanvi the Great* like a devoted foster father.

I don't think any of this would have been possible if I had waited for the screenplay to be locked before moving to the music stage. Such was the power of those melodies that they actually helped us carve out Tanvi Raina's character with complete clarity. The music supported the writing, rather than the other way around. We now had specific songs with us, and these needed to be woven (and not stitched) into the screenplay. These music sessions reiterated to me that if you want to create something extraordinary, it pays to break the assembly line!

7

Genuine Relationships Will Take You Far

With the music for the movie in place, the next crucial step was casting, and interestingly, I believe casting for the principal characters of #TTG was done decades ago—twenty to thirty years ago. Yes, it reads like a clickbait line, but it is not. It is the truth. Let me explain.

I was blessed to start at a time when face-to-face conversations were more prevalent than FaceTime calls. Messages were handwritten, not forwarded on WhatsApp. And the best way to wish someone on their achievements or important days was a long, warm hug. I am not going to rant like an old fellow criticising everything that has changed, but I am setting the context to remind you of the power of sincere, heartfelt bonds built over time. Knowing people in real terms is not the same as messaging them on their numbers or interacting through WhatsApp groups. You build stronger ties, deeper bonds, and longer-lasting, agenda-free friendships when you meet people face-to-face, visit their place, eat with them, invest your time and energy, and exchange words, experiences, ideas, and ideologies, over a cup of tea or meals.

I can make my point clearer with a very contemporary example. Observe what happens on your regular Zoom calls, which have become a part of the professional world since the Covid days. Some people come on camera, some don't but that is okay. The meeting starts on time, we greet each other, and after some basic pleasantries, we start discussing what is on the agenda. Whether these meetings have a pre-decided time limit or not, they end once the agenda is covered, and everyone just logs out. One feels more drained on these calls than in face-to-face meetings, and therefore, the disconnection feels like a relief.

Now compare this with a typical boardroom meeting where you go with your team or colleagues. You will settle in, greet each other, ask about well-being, and compliment one or two people for their sartorial tastes or appearances. During the meeting, the all-important question will arise: tea or coffee, green tea or black coffee, with or without sugar? You will discover the tastes and preferences of the group. Of course, the expert body language reader in you will also work overtime. And then, once the meeting ends, you will head to the nearest tea stall to discuss how the meeting went, and whether the main speaker was funny, boring, weird, sharp, rude, or just plain ridiculous, depending on how much spice you like in your gossip. These are the toppings on the base of physical meetings. All in all, you really get to know people so much better this way.

The same thing happened in our industry. When I started as an actor, the cool vanity vans were fewer and hearts were warmer. So, between shots, we actually spent a lot more time with our colleagues, gossiping, playing cards or chess, pulling pranks, or diving into deep conversations about life and worldviews (depending, of course, on the intellectual bandwidth of the group). This is the reason why many colleagues generally ended up becoming friends and sometimes, even like family. This is not rocket science; I am just stating the fundamentals of human behaviour. The time and energy you spend being good to people and being their true friend pays off eventually, and it pays off handsomely. The casting of *Tanvi the Great* (for roles other than Tanvi Raina's) is an example of this fact.

My dear friend, Satish Kaushik, was the first actor with whom I shared this idea in late 2022. He had really liked the subject back then. However, by mid-2023, the screenplay that began taking shape was totally different and fresh. Never, in our writing sessions, did we even faintly try to write any of the characters with an actor in mind. The characters led us, scene after scene. Neither market forces nor personal equations ever factored in—not even for a second—when we were building the characters that the world will see in the film. As the filmmaker, all I hoped (and secretly prayed for) was that only those who would truly appreciate the essence of the story, the purity of Tanvi Raina's world, and value the passion that led me to return to the director's chair, would become part of this film.

However, the dilemma that emerged in my head was like this: While I didn't want to buckle under any pressure or influence for the casting, I also didn't have unlimited funds to approach actors who perfectly fit the role but came with a hefty price tag. So, the question lingered—would I still manage to get the perfect cast?

As shared earlier, one prominent producer-director had recommended a very sweet-looking, 'safe' actress for the lead role. I would have been sitting on a cushioned budget had I agreed to that suggestion. But this film was my Dandi March, and I had to make my own salt.

The dilemma playing out in my head was this: while I didn't want to buckle under any pressure or outside influence when it came to casting my actors, I also didn't have endless funds to rope in those actors whose fees matched how perfect they were for the role. So, would I be able to get the perfect cast? Meanwhile, as someone still practising the dying art of staying in touch without an agenda, I continued dropping by to meet friends just to say a simple 'Hi' or 'Hello'. On one such round of visits, I caught up with my friends and colleagues Anil Kapoor, Jackie Shroff, and Boman Irani, and told them I had decided to don the director's hat again. All of them were quite happy and encouraging. In fact, Shroff felt I had taken a bit too long to return to direction.

By this time, the screenplay had placed the protagonist, Tanvi Raina, in the company of mature men—characters hardened in their beliefs by time and experience. Naturally, this created space for seasoned actors in the film. Hence, I felt it was essential to contrast the actress playing Tanvi with stalwarts of cinema.

Our line producer, Aditya Shastry, had worked out a ballpark production budget of INR 45 crores, which was a challenging figure for Anupam Kher Studios. Our friend from the shipping industry had pledged only INR 25 crores. So, the question of whether we could afford to bring my actor friends on board didn't have a very promising answer. Still, the film had a heartbeat of its own, and word about it quietly began to travel among close friends.

One day, Shroff came home and asked how the film was coming along. I told him the screenplay was shaping up in a way that inspired me every single day. A couple of more questions later, I ended up narrating the entire script to him and telling him how it was important for me, personally, to bring back the cinema of innocence we all grew up watching during the good old days.

Shroff is an emotionally driven man—a fact as well-known as the sun rising in the East. With moist eyes and a choked voice, he declared that he wanted to be a part of this film. I told him we were still working on the funds. Shroff looked into my eyes for what felt like a long, intense minute and softly said, '*Maine maange paise tere se? Jab honge, tab de dena.*' (Did I ask you for money? Pay me when you can.) As I tried to absorb his magnanimity, he gave a slightly more reasonable reply that money was not the reason he wanted to do this film. At that stage, the character he would eventually play was not well-developed, which made my hesitation grow in direct proportion to his keenness. But I wondered, if it wasn't the money and the role, then what could his motivation be? I asked him why he wanted to be a part of the film, and his answer left me with tears in my eyes. He explained that he wanted to be part of this film, which is centred around goodness and innocence because he sought a kind of catharsis. The story, he said, was calling him to cleanse his soul—a detoxifying experience he was eager to embrace. His answer meant the world to me, as it revealed that I had found someone who truly saw Tanvi's world in the exact way it was meant to be seen.

Along with Jackie, I had also reached out to Boman Irani, who had gained significant recognition as a screenplay writing teacher through his online scriptwriting classes, Spiralbound, to spare some time for me. I wanted his free consultation along with some authentic but free *akoori* (a Parsi dish). Boman generously provided both. He offered valuable tips and shared a few points of admiration for the script.

On my way back home, looking at the extra akoori that Zenobia, Boman's affectionate wife, had packed, I questioned myself—how had I not found a role for Boman in the film yet? This realisation hit me, and I knew the least I could do was speak to him regarding this. I could have called him immediately, but you cannot insult an authentic akoori from an actual Parsi kitchen. I honoured it by polishing it off before finally calling Boman. He jokingly said that whatever

Zenobia had mixed in the akoori had worked! I 'un-joked' the situation by telling him that I was still working on the finances. What he said in response was strikingly similar to Jackie's response: 'Did I ask you for money, Kher saab? Pay me whenever you are comfortable.' With his usual warmth, he added that he would love to be part of the film, especially to be there for a friend calling the shots on set after twenty-two years. He wanted to do this film as a gesture of his support because he could foresee that *Tanvi the Great* was not an easy film to make! 'Dost lagenge, Kher saab,' he said before ending the call.

Boman is a very passionate man. I have known him as a friend since the days of *Khosla Ka Ghosla*, which was Dibakar Banerjee's debut film. Years of stardom had not eroded Boman's goodness, not even by .00001 mm. I was truly grateful to have him as part of this film.

Both Boman's and Shroff's warmth and unwavering support reminded me just how much strength old friendships bring to a journey like this. If I share the details of how another old friend agreed to be a part of this film without even charging a rupee as a signing amount or advance, the content may become repetitive. But this is exactly how it happened with my friend, Arvind Swamy!

Arvind is a man of many talents, including running a highly successful business of his own. Although we haven't collaborated on many films, our connection has remained strong since our work on *Saat Rang Ke Sapne*—the only film we did together back in the late 90s. We have stayed in touch ever since. I also make it a point to visit his home whenever I am in Chennai.

Arvind heard the story and found the role I had envisioned for him intriguing. But more than that, he wanted to stand by me because *Tanvi the Great* was going to be my first film as both producer and director. He said, 'You can pay me when you make profits after the release.' The confidence and faith he placed in me meant far more than any amount I could have ever transferred to his account.

However, things played out very differently when it came to casting the pivotal role of Tanvi's mother. I think I went through almost every name that topped the charts in the 1990s. Each of them listened patiently and showed genuine interest. But none of those conversations turned into a 'yes'. Most felt that the protagonist's role would overshadow theirs. One of them, a dear friend and one of the biggest stars of that era, simply went silent after our meeting. I waited for her call, but her name never lit up my phone.

Eventually, we bumped into each other at a common friend's party. She smiled sheepishly and confessed she wasn't sure how I would take a 'no'. I leaned in and whispered that the number of rejections for that role had already crossed double digits, so she didn't need to worry about it.

The way out of this labyrinth of rejections came through the door of a dear friend—veteran actor, director, and producer Pallavi Joshi. She loved the script, connected with it instantly, and saw the power and depth in the role. And if I may say so, the role of Tanvi's mother is one of those parts that can really lift an actor's career graph like an express elevator.

There was also this other scene—crucial and packed with emotion—that comes just before the climax. Although it was just one scene, I needed an actor with immense depth and gravitas to truly anchor it. Interestingly, we had never really discussed this role from an actor's perspective during the writing stage. Ironically, this was the scene that went through the most drafts, revised over months. It was only later that I began to envision the calibre of talent required to do justice to it.

Uncertain of the response—since it was, after all, a single-scene role—I reached out to Nassar, an actor with over 700 films to his name. His experience across a diverse range of films and languages brought remarkable strength to the scene. And once again, I found a friend in Nassar, someone who not only embraced the role with a profound sense of ownership but also nurtured it to a picture-perfect conclusion.

I am not sharing these anecdotes to highlight the film's star cast or to boast about signing them without the usual financial formalities. The point I am trying to make is that all this happened because of their genuine love for a friend who was about to learn to ride a new kind of bicycle, and they wanted to be there, steadying the handlebars, ensuring the ride was smooth and safe. This sentiment and heartfelt support would not have been possible without the existence of a strong, deep-rooted bond of friendship.

The truth is that relationships need to be cultivated, nourished, and nurtured. After all, they are not seasonal crops that have to be harvested; instead, they are thick shady trees that provide shelter from life's harshest weather. And to nurture a tree is no simple task. It needs effort and commitment. This is not possible through WhatsApp and emoji-led communication alone. This culture of transactional, need-based interactions might seem efficient or even professional, but professionals can't do for you what real friends can. That, for me, was the greatest lesson. This is also the reason why it is important to be honest, real, and sincere in relationships. When you decide to fly, your friends can become your wings and your parachute too!

8

Even the Greatest Paintings Begin with a Blank Canvas

Those who think they know the market forces often end up doing what the market forces them to do. That is why I do not blame my friends who suggested I either pre-sell this film to a top OTT platform or, at the very least, cast an actress who was already well-established in the titular role. These were well-wishers—friends, veterans, seasoned producers—who had seen every possible dimension of the film business. Their advice wasn't without merit, and to be fair, it came with a couple of teaspoons of genuine concern for me.

One of them—a completely self-made man who rose from the by-lanes of a small town on the sheer strength of his hard work—even suggested I drop the idea of making a film on this subject altogether. While his words didn't shake my faith in the film, I would be lying if I said they didn't stir me up. That night, I was unable to sleep properly. (To be honest, my average deep sleep is already lower than ideal, but for that night, I am happy to blame it entirely on that producer!)

The next morning, without stopping anywhere else, I went straight to his office. He wasn't expecting me, so he hadn't arrived yet. I waited for him, and when he finally walked in, I said just one thing to him: 'Producer bhai, you are neither my father nor do I owe anything to you. Feel free to say 'no' to financing this film and I shall understand. But please don't ask me not to make this film.' Needless to say, I walked out of his office even before the tea was served in his cabin.

I didn't do this to prove a point to him. It was to remind myself—and strongly so—that my bucket of resources may be empty, but that didn't mean I could allow that space to be filled with self-doubt. This story, so pure, so untouched by cynicism, deserved to be brought into the world.

I fully understood that all this was happening because everyone felt that making a film of such scale, with a newcomer in the lead, would not be prudent y during one of the most turbulent phases the film industry has seen. But then waves and phases are meant to pass. Moreover, being in the field of art for more than four decades, I have also come to realise that such a scenario is the ultimate test of a director's conviction and beliefs. And I was ready to pass this test with flying colours.

Life has taught me through ample live demos that gut feeling is, more often than not, a great feeling. It is far more accurate than exit polls. And my gut feeling told me, loud and clear, that Tanvi Raina had to be portrayed by a completely fresh face—someone the audience had never seen on screen before. The audience should not see even the faintest trace of an actress in her. Instead, they should be left wondering how we have managed to extract this performance from an actually autistic girl!

Here again, it was not about a director's creative ambition, but about the most organic, realistic enactment of the story. I had read somewhere: 'Only real stories or realistically portrayed stories change the world.' (That 'somewhere' turned out to be my own notepad. I had scribbled it myself!)

With this goal in mind, I started looking for a young girl who would have the tenderness and vulnerability that cannot be replicated by any artist. Those who have worked closely with me have often heard me say, '*Actor ko, acting ki acting nahin karni chahiye.*' (An actor should not put up a pretence of acting.) Fortunately, I did not have to go too far—both literally and figuratively—because the girl I was looking for, or perhaps I should say the girl who was destined and then born to become Tanvi Raina on screen, was honing her acting skills and nurturing her dream to be an actor in the hall right behind my room, at my very own acting school, Actor Prepares.

For the uninitiated, Actor Prepares is a world-class acting school I started two decades ago, in 2005, for aspiring actors from all over the country. We offer a range of programmes designed to train actors through intensive instruction, and I personally conduct masterclasses for every batch—a small gesture of gratitude to an industry that has given me everything I have today.

In one of the classes at Actor Prepares, I gave all the students a simple-sounding but complex-to-perform exercise. I told them to lie down in the foetal position with absolutely no expressions on their faces. No expression meant a totally blank face. As I walked around checking the face of every student, I found only one student who could achieve the desired calmness and peacefulness. It meant she had completely surrendered herself to the directions that were given. As I looked at her face, I caught an unmistakable glimpse of Tanvi Raina in her. This was Shubhangi Dutt—the girl the world would come to know as Tanvi Raina within a year.

Shubhangi had dreamt of becoming an actor since childhood. I shortlisted her along with two or three other girls for the auditions. I spoke to each of them—about their aspirations, backgrounds, and outlook on life—in an effort to understand who they truly were beyond the performance. Shubhangi stood out with her calm, composed demeanour. She came from a humble background and had faced life's challenges from a very young age, yet there wasn't the slightest trace of bitterness or glumness in her. She only spoke about what she planned to do in the future with a great sense of value for life. She also possessed a good sense of humour and mischievousness that suited her age. I did not realise it back then, but as I write this today, I see a striking similarity between her demeanour towards life—despite all the hardships she faced—and my own. This young lady also drew strength from everything life had given her so far, using it not to look back, but to keep moving forward. I felt she wasn't apologetic or hesitant when facing life head-on. She was a survivor who wanted to become an actor to change the fortune of her family. Until then, she had only appeared in a few ads here and there, but she was about to step into the spotlight in a way she never had before.

My gut feeling had already told me Shubhangi was the one, but my mind was conditioned to act like a righteous bureaucrat. So, while I did test a few others, I kept increasing the test levels for Shubhangi without ever letting her know what it was for. She would come up with her own interpretations, add her two bits to the given brief, and send me the video recordings. Occasionally, I showed her videos to my writers and Herman. All of us were impressed by her dedication and commitment. However, the body language of my writers—and it was even confirmed by them later—indicated they were only half-convinced by my choice. This wasn't entirely unexpected, as early on, even they had suggested a few established—or rather, experienced—actresses whom they believed were powerhouse performers and best suited for the role. However, I was searching for an actress who was more suitable than the most suitable one, and I had found her!

After a couple of months and watching several videos, I was sure that Shubhangi from my masterclass was the one. Her real commitment was put to the test when she was eventually chosen for the role. As shared earlier, I did not want people to see an actress playing Tanvi Raina. Instead, I wanted them to see a girl named Tanvi Raina playing herself in the film. For this, it was almost a prerequisite to keep her under wraps. She readily agreed to go off social media and not take any other acting assignment in any form. This is not an easy thing to do, and as an actor, I can vouch for it.

As someone from a generation that thrives on social media, Shubhangi certainly understood the challenge. To quote her, she had to go into 'MIA mode' (missing in action). But staying under the radar wasn't easy. While the rest of us moved about freely, she had to wear a bluish surgical mask or the N-95 mask—popular since the Covid days—whenever she stepped out with us, to avoid being photographed by passersby. We were invited to several dinners by army officers and other prominent figures in Lansdowne, where she had to politely decline when the hosts asked for a picture with her. She even had to do this for our own team photos and selfies!

Meanwhile, our 'producer' from the shipping industry kept asking about the actress playing the titular role. I told him about our discovery and how well she was performing. His reaction made it clear he would have preferred a more established name. But choosing someone new also meant taking on the responsibility of mentoring her—something far more demanding than most people realise.

Mentoring is not an easy task, and it is definitely not everyone's cup of tea. It requires as much dedication and faith from the mentor as it does from the person being mentored. In fact, at times, it tests not just your patience, but also your judgement and your conviction. A single crack in the mentor's confidence can shatter the protégée completely. Therefore, the mentor must constantly walk a fine line, balancing both responsibility and care.

I knew I wasn't just taking responsibility for someone's career, but also their dreams and aspirations. So, with all the work that was happening at the back end—scriptwriting, search for the department heads, financial agreements, location scouting, etc.—I would regularly slip into my role as the 'super teacher'. With every lesson and every session, I hoped and prayed that Shubhangi would transform into Tanvi Raina with such perfection that even her own folks would be tempted to apply for a change of her name on her Aadhaar Card! At the end of the day, all our efforts—not just financial, but emotional and creative too—were riding on her tall shoulders. And that is the most I can reveal about her for now!

From acting workshops to regimented workouts, from dance classes to in-depth sessions on understanding autism, her schedule was packed to the brim, leaving not a single minute to spare. And as a final test-cum-prep work, I decided to send this Tanvi to Tezpur, where the real Tanvi Anand, my niece, lived with her parents in the cantonment area. She was supposed to spend about eight to ten days with the real Tanvi, befriending and observing her.

Though this may sound like method acting, it was anything but that. I had no interest in cloning or mimicking the real Tanvi. What I wanted was for the on-screen Tanvi

Raina to absorb the energy and the aura of Tanvi Anand. As abstract or even absurd as that may sound, I truly believe it happened.

And then, on 16 February 2024, when the camera finally rolled for *Tanvi the Great* and Shubhangi appeared in front of it for the very first time, she blew us away. She floored us. Mouths fell open and jaws dropped. And as we would soon come to realise, that moment was just the tip of the iceberg.

Here, I must also give credit to our brilliant styling team, led by the super-talented stylist Rohit Chaturvedi. They worked meticulously to transform this young girl from Mumbai into the distinctively adorable innocent and innocent-looking Tanvi Raina, crafting every detail of her physical appearance with care and precision.

Day after day, scene after scene, this cub learnt to roar in front of the camera. In almost every scene, Shubhangi was pitted against veterans, the giants of the industry, and yet, she stood her ground like a true lead actor, armed with complete innocence, dedication, and relentless hard work. In her own words, she was a lamb surrounded by lions. But with every performance, the pride of lions began to love her, much like how Mowgli was embraced by his jungle pack!

Now, you might wonder how all this was even possible. Of course, it was the girl's talent, commitment, and hard work that put her in that position. But just as important was the environment we built around her which significantly contributed to her performance and allowed her to truly shine.

My experience tells me that having an actor as your first director is a huge advantage, and in Shubhangi's case, it worked out beautifully. I knew exactly what kind of challenges she must have been going through. As someone with over 540 films behind me—easily five hundred times more experience than her—I had a fair idea of what would make her job not just easier, but sharper too.

I observed her performance the way a microbiologist studies a specimen under a microscope—closely, curiously, carefully. I made mental notes and came up with techniques to draw out her best. We did workshops and rehearsals together, where I acted out every line and every scene to help her discover the hidden potential in each moment. My feedback was constant and my patience, persistent. I needed her to play a diffident girl with confidence.

Moreover, from day one, I made it a point to sensitise every member of the crew—not only because we were tackling a delicate subject, but also because our lead actor was still wet behind the ears. Therefore, I asked everyone to be gentle, soft-spoken, and compassionate in their interactions. I did this because I knew very well that the tone of the work environment flows from the top, like a river. And if I am being honest, maintaining that kind of environment consistently is no easy task!

Soon enough, Abhishek and Ankur, who were easily twenty years older than Shubhangi, became her closest buddies! In fact, she would pull their legs, crack jokes over meals, and keep the laughter flowing. (And yes, we all ate together—none of that vanity van isolation here.) She even gave the writer duo a nickname: 'Dholu-Bholu'!

From the makeup and costume teams to Kruti Mahesh, our choreographer, and the Ads, everyone was a friend to her. No surprise then that she was in tears on the last day of our Lansdowne schedule. After all, she had found a family away from home for nearly a month and a half.

Of course, no one had a clue—but now you know—about the kind of stress we were under as a production house during the Lansdowne shoot! I was reeling under financial pressure and Herman had started looking at least two years older. Thankfully, everyone just assumed it was the sunburn from the mountains that made him look a bit worn out.

But the truth is that the real hero of the shoot was Shubhangi. She had become the *laadli bachchi* (beloved girl) of the entire crew. Not once did anyone see her flustered or under any kind of pressure even before the most demanding scenes, and trust me, there were many—both emotionally as well as physically. She would come prepared on the set with every line etched into her heart, ready to blossom on cue, much to the joy of her director!

Mentoring is a selfless responsibility that demands more from the mentor than from the one being mentored. I truly believe her DNA would have matched with that of Tanvi Raina, if she existed in real life.

I probably wouldn't have faced the financial crunch just before the shoot if I had listened to the well-meaning advice about casting someone more experienced or better known. But to accomplish something extraordinary, your inner voice of belief has to be louder than all the voices of naysayers put together.

All in all, it wasn't a smooth ride from day one—for either the director or the actor. Naturally, there were days tougher than others, and scenes that tested both my faith and Shubhangi's talent. But then, there is no real sense of achievement if you take an elevator or a chopper to the summit of Mt. Everest. The glory lies in the climb, one step at a time. That is how I worked with Shubhangi. I would sit down with her, point out areas for improvement, acknowledge her strengths, and help her confront her fears and vulnerabilities, reassuring her that she wasn't taking the plunge alone, without a guide. Remember that sincere effort always pays off, and in this case, the cub learnt to roar—sometimes louder than the lions.

9

Not Everything Is in Your Hands—Destiny Plays Its Part Too

Sometimes, it is a blessing when the road ahead gets blocked because you might just stumble upon another path, one even more beautiful. That is exactly what happened when I was searching for someone with the vision to see my dream and capture it so exquisitely that it felt like a dream itself. The way our director of photography (DoP) came on board was nothing short of providence.

With my ancestral roots tracing back to Kashmir and my childhood blooming in Shimla—the capital of Himachal Pradesh, nestled in the heart of the majestic Himalayas—I am a mountain boy right down to my bone marrow. Growing up in Shimla, which then served as the Western Command Headquarters of the Indian Army, I developed a deep and lasting affinity for the armed forces. I suspect there was some quiet leakage from the memory stock of my subconscious mind when I began searching for an apt storyline for *Tanvi the Great*, and there is a reason I believe that.

Even before the plot had taken any concrete shape, I knew the story would be set in the mountains. I began getting vivid flashes of a small but picturesque hill station—not one overrun by tourists but rather, a serene, tucked-away place. I could see men in uniform walking down roads lined with verdant green slopes, and snowcapped peaks glowing golden under the early morning sun. It had to be a quaint, quiet town that had managed to preserve its charm since the colonial era.

Meanwhile, our writer Abhishek came up with the unusual name of a lesser-known hill station in the mountain state of Uttarakhand as the place where the story could unfold and be filmed, too. It was a place he had heard about often from his childhood friend in Lucknow. For him, it was as exotic as Shangri-La. When he suggested the name Lansdowne, he also showed me some stunning pictures of the town on his phone. I was stunned the moment I saw them. They so closely resembled the quaint and quiet army town I had been visualising for months in my mind! It felt familiar, as if I had known this place all along. Within minutes and after a quick round of deliberation, we declared that Tanvi Raina's grandfather, Col Pratap Raina, lives in Lansdowne! But imagining a place is one thing; capturing its soul on camera is another, and that is where the role of the DoP became absolutely crucial.

It is not hard to imagine how critical the role of the DoP was in *Tanvi the Great*. After all, the world sees what the director envisions only through the eyes of the DoP. To visualise a destination or a dream is one thing—even a few pegs can help with that! But finding team members who share that vision and can see it as vividly as you do—that is the real test of leadership. Four blind people trying to describe an elephant by touching different parts can never paint an accurate picture. Singularity of vision is key to any success.

Since my approach to filmmaking was a little different from the norm, working on this film became both a creative challenge and a journey for the DoP. But before anyone assumes that this difference stemmed from some deep, esoteric, or lofty creative world view, let me clarify—it was mostly because I wasn't a conventionally trained, reference-inspired director. My storytelling was going to be inspired by life and governed by the heart: simple, real, and without a dull moment. Also, one of the things that I believe was singular to my way of filmmaking was that I did not take the beaten path of regimental adherence to breakdowns and storyboards, which to my mind—no offence meant to those who do a great job of it—belong more to a physics class than to cinema.

We did a thorough recce of each and every location and absorbed the scenes in great detail, but I did not let our shot breakdowns become my blinkers. I did not strangulate my intuitive voice, as more often than not, it kept giving me innovative suggestions that made things better and clearer in my head. After all, we had travelled all the way to the somewhat remote location of Lansdowne so that we could come back with a very realistic, fresh-looking film. It would have been a disservice to our vision had we closed our minds instead of drawing inspiration from the gorgeous surroundings.

I believe vision and ambition are first cousins. They love to stay together, and one fosters the other. That is why it should sound more obvious than pompous when I say that I was sure I wanted to make an international-looking film—the kind of cinema the audience lauds as world cinema. Indian films in world cinema have usually been about poverty and the struggle of the impoverished. There are hardly any international Indian films that are about normal human relationships or the conflicts within a family. I thought my film should break the shackles of the economic impressions that our cinema has been tagged with for decades.

All this reads good and stimulating, right? But now think about the DoP, who had to shoot all of it in an eight-hour shift, in a season and geography where the sun is not contractually bound to adhere to your eight hours! Thus, we needed a DoP who not only shared our filmmaking vision but could also take on the film's challenges head-on. Naturally, that kind of ambition knows no borders, and so my search for the right DoP took me beyond India.

I saw showreels, movies, and shows, consulted my directors and colleagues in Hollywood, spoke to some agents, and finally dialled the number of a DoP with a memorable name: Keiko Nakahara. As it is easy to guess by her name, Keiko is from Japan. She has accumulated good exposure to varied kinds of cinema, working with some of the most talented directors across the globe.

I really liked Keiko's work. Her colour palette has a distinctive touch of tenderness. She had also done some noticeable Indian movies, and her work was impressive. So, we got in touch with her and found out that she was in her homeland at that time. She was quite clear about her working style, expectations, and schedule. Her forthright approach seemed like an added advantage.

Our line producer, Aditya Shastri, had by then worked out the numbers and the schedule. Somehow, Keiko's travel plans and our schedule did not match. Such situations are not unusual in our industry, especially while dealing with talent that is in great demand. So, we had no choice but to move on.

The film was about warm-hearted people in the cold mountains. It needed to capture the innocence of the characters and the beauty of the terrain in equal measure. I interacted with a couple of more DoPs and chose one who, just a year ago, had done a film set in the Himalayas with me. His work looked really clean and good on screen. The man had also shot scores of good-looking ad films over the years.

Though not exactly famous for his cool temperament, his work displayed a streak of freshness and, in his demeanour, an element of eagerness to be a part of Tanvi's universe. We had discussions about the film and life in general. I found him thoughtful and a borderline philosopher too. During our interactions, at home and at the office, I also discovered that he had experienced the rough edges of life quite closely. This gave him an augmented sensitivity and emotional rawness. He even shared an idea for a short film or video on loneliness and how it can be neutralised with pet adoption; he wished to shoot it with me. I was happy that I had found yet another key member of the team. Getting the right DoP is akin to getting a 20/20 vision for the director, especially when the director is originally an actor, returning to the director's chair for only the second time after more than two decades! For those who do not know much about the filmmaking process, I must explain that it is the DoP who plays an influential—sometimes even decisive—role in the choice of location, lights, and other related equipment, thereby eventually affecting the shooting schedule as well as the budget. Given the DoP's central role and the close collaboration required on set, I believe it is important that we share not just a professional understanding, but a deeper sense of camaraderie.

I like to take people along with me in a horizontal line—all moving together, shoulder-to-shoulder, like a wave—and not as a vertical column, one behind the other. Therefore, I like to believe that when we come together to spend fifty, sixty, or perhaps a hundred days together, we should bond like one big family, where we know about each other as much as we know about our family members or close friends. So, when our newly appointed DoP made me speak to his family members over a video call, I took it as a measure of his level of involvement and passion for this film.

The production team, always eager to make budgets as soon as anything new is even discussed, got down to work and chalked out the required finances according to the inputs given by the DoP. Not long after, I even made a short trip to Lansdowne with the DoP to familiarise myself with the place and to familiarise the authorities there with our requirements. This was an emotional day for me. In Lansdowne, not only did I see the perfect location for bringing Tanvi's world alive but also made the first formal trip for recce and a dummy shoot with the DoP. The results were dreamy because winter was just around the corner and it had sent fog ahead of it, as its harbinger.

I still can't tell whether I was emotionally excited or excitedly emotional when I shared those photos and clips across all our department WhatsApp groups. Everyone loved what the DoP had captured through his lenses. This was sometime in October, and we were supposed to start rolling in February. Since I was going to be the director with limited experience calling the shots on a film set, I needed to sit down with my DoP to finalise shots and clearly understand how we would treat the scenes, at least a month before the shoot. By all standards, it was a fair plan.

Following my 'moving-like-a-wave-and-not-a-column' instincts, I was in no mood to dictate anything to anyone. As an individual and as an artist, I value a democratic environment and that was the case even when I hadn't played

Dr Manmohan Singh and Jai Prakash Narayan. So, I called up the DoP to figure out his dates for our pre-production discussions. Meanwhile, we had also planned a table read of the script sometime in January. (Since our producers were still on board at the time, the event was conducted in a formal and somewhat ceremonious manner.) But to my surprise, the DoP expressed his inability to spare time and be available for this exercise. I wondered what could be keeping him away from such crucial preparation work. He said he had to travel to the UK for a few days. The absence of such a key person in the team can unnerve even a captain as cool as Mahendra Singh Dhoni.

This unavailability and the UK clause were news to me. The DoP maintained that he had informed us earlier. However, neither I nor Herman could recall any such conversation or chat. I won't call it a stalemate, because we weren't supposed to play against each other; rather, we had agreed to create something special, tender, and unique. So as a director, I felt that the glasses through which I had started seeing the film were suddenly snatched away from me! It seemed that whatever the DoP had to attend to was pretty urgent and could not be rescheduled. It had to be! We soon learnt that it was a multi-starrer project based on an Italian film and to the DoP, it seemed like a bigger opportunity than ours. He had signed up for this film, parts of which were scheduled to be shot in the UK right around the same time we were set to begin preparations for *Tanvi the Great*.

I have reason to believe that my sleep is severely allergic to stress and predicaments. The moment it finds me in a difficult spot, it stops paying me a visit! It happened on this occasion too. I was worried because, as explained earlier, much of the logistics at the shoot are governed by the director–DoP partnership. Additionally, I knew what differentiates a success story from any other is the right blend of passion and commitment. Just like a drink made from the concentrate of fruit pulp isn't the same as pure juice, half-measures and half-attention, even when served with full honesty, do not yield the same results as when one works with complete focus.

Another key factor was that the film's subject was both unique and sensitive. The location we had chosen for the shoot was unexplored, with numerous rules to consider. This was the first time Anupam Kher Studios, as a production house, was handling an entire production of this scale. The cast featured highly experienced professionals, each with limited time. And on top of all this, an actor with relatively little experience in filmmaking was in the driving seat. The situation, while not exactly intimidating, was quite challenging indeed.

In such a scenario, it seemed risky to have a DoP dividing his time and energy between two projects. The dilemma was real, and the DoP himself acknowledged it. We weighed the situation objectively and, with heavy hearts, decided to part ways, even as the planning for the shoot was in full swing.

Before I tell you what happened next, let me ask you something: how would you feel if you suddenly lost your vision? Take a pause and think. Your answer is more or less how I felt when we made this tough call. Losing your DoP at such an advanced stage of pre-production can be a challenge even for seasoned filmmakers. And I was only a few shades more than a newcomer in terms of direction! But it was better to part ways at this stage than to continue at a pace that wouldn't match. And so, just when we were ready to begin shooting, we found ourselves back in search mode once again!

By this point, I was convinced that the film needed a gentle soul on set—someone with a strong aesthetic sense, a deep well of empathy and kindness, and a calm presence to steady the anxiety and urgency that often accompany a shoot. My brief conversations with Keiko had left me with the feeling that she might just be that person. And now that we were once again searching for a DoP, I decided to reach out to her again.

I called her up, but she didn't answer. Why she didn't answer my call turned out to be one of those moments that felt like divine intervention. There I was, reaching out to Keiko to see if she could take on a film about the autistic granddaughter of a retired army officer, and there she was, sitting in a doctor's clinic in Japan with her 18-month-old son. The doctor had just handed her a diagnosis that shook her to the core.

Overwhelmed and unsettled, Keiko returned home with a mind full of questions and fears, especially as a single parent. Her eyes stayed fixed on her son, who was laughing and playing, blissfully unaware of what the doctor had just said. Her sister, her greatest pillar of strength, handed her the phone. And despite everything she was going through, despite her thoughts being pulled in a dozen directions, Keiko—true to her deep-rooted professionalism—called me back the moment she saw the missed call.

After the customary but sincere exchange of greetings, I told Keiko that our shooting dates had shifted by a few weeks, and it would be wonderful if she could take on the film. She nonchalantly asked what the film was about. As soon as I mentioned that it was about an autistic girl, Keiko immediately said yes.

I was relieved and happy. I quickly launched into my gratitude speech, expressing how excited I was to team up with her. She accepted my gratitude with the humility so characteristic of Japanese culture. As I pictured her bowing repeatedly while speaking—true to tradition—she gently surprised me by explaining, in just ninety seconds, why she had said yes to *Tanvi the Great*.

She told me that her son had just been diagnosed as autistic. There was a pause—a cinematic 'beat'—as her words sank in. I fell silent. Then she added that she saw this film as God's way of helping her understand autism more deeply. What she would learn through the making of this film, she believed, would guide her in raising her son, who had received his diagnosis barely an hour earlier.

About forty days later, I shared this story with Ankur and Abhishek during our final writing camp in December 2023. My voice quivered, and my eyes welled up. One of them was speechless, and the other stood with his jaw dropped (I can't recall who reacted how, but the moment was unforgettable). It was an uncanny coincidence—truly the mother of all coincidences. And before I could say it, the writers did—it was God's will that this film be made. There couldn't have been a more direct message or blessing than this! I couldn't have agreed more. To this day, this incident gives me goosebumps and fills my soul with a deep sense of gratitude to the Almighty. No pay cheque in the world could have brought me a DoP with such a profoundly personal and soulful reason for joining this project.

Now that I have brought up the cheque—though inadvertently—this episode had another significantly positive effect. By this point, we were just forty to forty-five days away from the shoot. I had been trying to get in touch with our shipping producer, as it was time for him to start transferring at least a portion of the funds he had committed. But the gentleman kept avoiding my calls. When he finally responded, his explanation for the delay was nothing but a series of excuses. From being summoned by the Income Tax Department to last-minute board meetings, he always had a solid reason to avoid discussing the funds transfer. It felt like he was sending excuses the way people send email attachments: PFA Reason No. 12. It was December, and while it felt like Christmas had arrived, my Santa hadn't.

The truth is that a delay like this would have made anyone shiver and lose their nerve. But the way divine intervention connected a mother of a toddler in the Far East with me and my film gave me a surge of unshakable faith and courage. Despite the looming financial crunch Herman and I were facing, I was certain I had been chosen to tell the story of a young autistic girl chasing an impossible dream.

However, the mounting financial uncertainty, coupled with a change of DoP at such a critical juncture, brought its own set of challenges. Keiko's approach required assistants, lighting, and equipment that differed significantly from what we had originally budgeted for, putting additional strain on our finances. But sometimes, in the pursuit of excellence, you have to ignore what the first five letters of the word 'budget' are telling you to do! This insight isn't merely a product of my own cleverness (though, admittedly, that is part of it); it is rooted in the confidence of someone who has been immersed in cinema for over four decades, closely observing some of the greatest filmmakers at work. When the world watches the film, it will become evident why Keiko's frames were the perfect fit for this project. With minimalist lighting, a daily dose of Japanese green tea (which, I must confess, twisted my tongue every time I tried to pronounce it), and a deeply nurtured understanding of the film's soul, she created pure magic. The upheaval we experienced was, in the end, absolutely worth it.

In India, we live by the belief that 'if all is not well, it will eventually get well' because we understand that success isn't solely a result of our goodness or efficiency but also because someone up there wants our plans to succeed and our dreams to be realised. Of course, we must do our best, remain honest, and stay optimistic in our efforts. But it is always helpful to remember that there is always a little space for destiny in everything we do.

10

Sometimes, It Is Good to Have Your Back Against the Wall

Sometimes I wonder if God enjoys playing *Super Mario*—probably the most popular video game the world knew before PUBG came along—with us in His free time. Obstacles keep popping up one after the other and just like in the game, we are expected to keep moving forward as halting is not an option. We may have to break walls with our heads, jump, pound, punch, or even shoot our way through—in short, do whatever it takes to inch closer to the goal. But stopping? That is not on the table, not as long as there is life in you.

The challenges had been manageable so far, as things always seemed to work out one way or another, but it felt like God had now decided to test me at the highest level as we moved forward.

So, back to the point from where I began this sojourn into the pre-production days. Pranit informed me that the accommodation and ID cards were ready. I heard him out with only partial attention as my mind was elsewhere.

My—or for that matter, any producer's—worst fear was about to come true. The industrialist (let's call him Mr Sailor, since he was in the shipping business too, as mentioned earlier) had been keeping his communication with me to the bare minimum, as if his doctor had suddenly warned him that talking to me was bad for his gut health!

Mr Sailor had committed to investing INR 25 crores in our film. It was the lion's share, and I had planned to raise another INR 10 to 15 crores to somewhat match the budget proposed by Mr Shastry. Everything was on paper, and we had even registered a company to ensure complete clarity and compliance with every legal requirement. What I hadn't foreseen was that it would all remain just that: on paper. Nothing had entered our joint account yet.

Still, since the commitment had come from the well-regarded Mr Sailor, I thought I had no reason to worry. By this time, I had already incurred substantial expenses across departments. Around 180 people had been paid from my side. I don't mention this as a complaint as of course they had to be paid, and as the producer, it was my responsibility to ensure that. I bring it up only to highlight that my own share of the contribution was depleting faster than the glaciers of Antarctica. Yet, I never wanted a single person to feel they were being taken for granted.

So, after weeks of waiting, I finally sent a direct message to Mr Sailor on 10 December 2023, expressing the hope that he would release the promised funds without further delay. After all, we had made all our preparations and hired people not on the basis of an assumption, but on a firm commitment from him. However, what I received was a delayed response, not the fulfilment of a professionally made commitment.

This delayed response came in the form of an assurance. But who said the word 'assurance' is always a sign of something positive? In this case, it simply assured me that something was off. I began to wonder what truth lay beneath the evasions and vague replies.

Let's take a quick trivia break: Have you ever had the opportunity to relish the *bhelpuri* (a popular Indian snack) of patience and excitement? Yes, it may sound like an oxymoron, but while I was excited to proceed to the shoot, I was also being infinitely patient with Mr Sailor.

As the days passed, however, the crunch in this bhelpuri started to feel more like grit in my teeth. Merry Christmas messages were duly exchanged, along with the customary 'May your . . .' New Year messages in the last week of December. By now, with these delayed responses, I was sure either his signals or his intentions had gone weak! Otherwise, if not the whole, a part of the committed sum would have arrived by now. Or at the very least, a message or a call reassuring me that there was no major reason to worry should have come through.

Finally, the cover of pretence was blown off on the auspicious day of Lohri/Makar Sankranti (13 January 2024). And just for your information, our *mahurat* shot was scheduled to roll on 16 February! Mr Sailor admitted that the ship of partnership we had together set sail on had turned out to be a Titanic—there was a hole in it. He informed us that partners/board of directors had refused to approve the investment in the film industry.

Anyone who has dealt with business entities—big or small—knows that this board/partners line is like Mahendra Singh Dhoni's helicopter shot; it looks odd but is technically not out of the rule book. In Mr Sailor's case, his board could have easily come up with a more reasonable decision—like reducing the funds—instead of refusing it altogether. But they straightaway went with the now fashionable 'no means no' rule.

That meeting with Mr Sailor brought a flood of memories to the surface—the videos he once asked me to shoot with his family, the meals we shared, and the congratulatory messages we exchanged when the company was formed. All of it came rushing back, All of it came rushing back, almost as if to mock me. The truth was, the carpet was suddenly pulled from under our feet, and we found ourselves with our backs against the wall. Months of endeavour, hundreds of man-hours, and of course, my reputation—everything was at stake. And there was no way Herman or I could have let this news out. And there was no way I could have made the film any other way than how I had envisioned it—on a grand canvas, with an even grander heart.

I have never used the victim card in my life, not even in the most adverse situations. That is simply because I refused to be victimised. Adversities are like sunshine; they fall on everyone, and the only way to escape them is to be buried under the earth. How you respond to them decides whether you are a victim or a fighter. Even losing is a privilege reserved only for those who dare to fight. At the age of sixty-nine, much like my character in *Vijay 69*, I chose to fight. This fight stemmed from my belief that only extraordinary solutions can tackle extraordinary problems.

So, we sat down and calculated the minimum amount we required to begin the long outdoor schedule. The gap between Mumbai and Lansdowne was huge, and we didn't have the resources to bridge it, even when I decided to pull out additional funds from my savings. But then the sun of hope, like the actual sun, rose from the east. Odisha, to be precise. Someone came forward to invest INR 5 crores, and that seemed like a much needed lifeline. And though I wasn't entirely comfortable, I reluctantly agreed to latch onto that parachute of sorts. It helped get things moving again—the wheels were turning smoothly, no longer squeaking.

With my communication skills, body of work, and experience, convincing Mr Sailor's board or partners to reconsider their decision wouldn't have been an impossible task. But I didn't want to waste even an ounce of energy arguing with Mr Sailor or trying to change his mind. From my writers to the legendary Oscar winner Kreem Sir, to Keiko, and my principal actors—no one had to be convinced to come on board. They heard the outline, understood the heart of the story, and instantly expressed their desire to be part of this pristine world. So, I didn't want anyone who needed convincing to come on board.

All this sounds great, right? A typical hero-like approach. But there was a reason I chose the analogy of *Super Mario* over that of a superhero at the beginning of this chapter. Just about ten days before our first shot, the rising sun of hope from Odisha set all too soon. Our angel investor backed out, expressing his inability to provide the promised INR 5 crores. And just like that, we were back to square one.

That evening, sitting alone in the office, I was watching army training reference videos to plan the training sequence for *#TTG*. That is when I came across a clip of army jawans building a Burma bridge as a stopgap arrangement to cross a river stream. And that was it—the solution struck me. If we couldn't build a full-fledged bridge, we could at least build a Burma bridge!

I reached out to a few NRI friends in New York—connections I had made while living there during the shoot of *New Amsterdam*. Some of them were in investment banking. They listened to me, my journey, and the story of my film. I am still not sure what moved them more—my pitch or the story itself—but the silver lining was that they came together to contribute enough crores to get the shoot of *Tanvi the Great* underway. I only wish I had the words to express my gratitude in the measure it truly deserves. Later on, a banker from Delhi also chipped in with a couple of crores more.

But was it really that simple? Of course not. Before this happened, Herman had seriously considered postponing the shoot until we secured adequate funding. But I believed that dreams are too delicate to withstand the wear and tear of time. I refused to let any negative thoughts enter my mind and chose instead to fight.

In a strange way, this false hope of funds had actually helped us prepare for the scale I wanted to make this film on. We never once thought about profits or margins. My sole focus was on telling the story with the utmost honesty and integrity. In hindsight, perhaps this was God's way of preparing us for something exceptional. This false sense of financial security gave me the mental space to stay immersed in the creative process. Otherwise, I might have been forced to pause this process and go out searching for the money instead. In other words, since we couldn't find the boat, we learnt to swim. And the simple reason I could do all this was that when your back is against the wall, there is nowhere left to go but forward.

11

You Can't Win a Game You Don't Enjoy

Finally, the moment arrived for the dream to take shape. The shooting began on 16 February 2024 in Mysore Colony, Mumbai. Only Herman and I knew how we had managed to come this far. Walking on thin ice, tightrope balancing, playing with fire—every idiom that signifies putting your life or reputation at stake echoed through my mind, heart, and soul. Yet, the thrill of a new day, a fresh beginning, has always been my greatest inspiration. It is why I keep count of every film I act in.

The shortage of funds remained a very real challenge, but I knew it was time to keep that battle to myself. My priority was to ensure that the energy on set reflected the purity and beauty of Tanvi Raina's world that we had envisioned. It was extremely crucial to create an atmosphere of positivity and camaraderie. There was no way I would allow financial pressure to affect my behaviour, spirit, or the mood on set.

Now, let's take a quick pause and try to imagine the mental state of someone who has been on a roller-coaster ride like mine over the past few weeks!

At the age of sixty-nine, I had stepped out from the comfort of an air-conditioned vanity van—not as a senior, established actor enjoying his privileges, but as the commander-in-chief on the sultry, chaotic battlefield of filmmaking. This time, I wasn't a mercenary following orders; I was the one making the calls that would shape at least a year of nearly a hundred people's lives. It felt like walking into a massive BYOD (bring your own doubt) party, where everyone was ready to question your choices and decisions, while you yourself arrived with your own collection of personal self-doubts. But in order to come so far, I had overcome every bit of self-doubt and refused to be swayed neither by budget constraints nor by the conventional rulebooks of success. In fact, more coincidences and miracles had unfolded around me than in a Manmohan Desai script! My belief was firm that the most renewable and sustainable source of energy on this planet is our own passion. However, just when I thought I had enough material to fuel fifty TED Talks, life threw its greatest teacher in my path—betrayal.

Betrayal is like that tough physical training instructor (PTI) we all had in school. It pushes you to your limits, makes you sweat and struggle, but eventually leaves you stronger. I had placed my trust in people's promises and commitments to support my dream only to be let down at the eleventh hour. And the fact is that dressing it up as a 'nothing personal, just business' decision doesn't soften the blow.

Deals fall through. People change their minds. Markets shift. But being told there is no parachute in your backpack just as you are about to jump out of the chopper is such an extreme situation that even Red Bull wouldn't dare to sponsor it. On top of it all, memories of the early 2000s, when I had lost almost my entire fortune back due to a miscalculated television production venture, were not making matters any easier for me. I wasn't scared, but I was sharply aware of what I had gone through two decades ago. There are painkillers for a headache and balms for a sore body, but no remedy exists for a mind weighed down by past wounds. And this was the state I was in when I stepped into the beautiful, pure, and innocent world of Tanvi Raina, with a dagger lodged in my back, its tip missing the spine of my self-belief by just a few millimetres.

But no matter the challenges, I was absolutely clear about one thing—I had to maintain a positive work environment and keep everyone's morale high on set. So, on the first day of the shoot, outside the bungalow in Mysore Colony, I stood on an apple box and addressed the entire unit. I thanked them for being part of the journey and made one simple request: for the next couple of months, no shouting, no tantrums, and no petty politics. I told them that this was a film about a girl with a mindset as delicate as a dry leaf. A newcomer was playing the lead. I needed everyone to bring empathy, kindness, and honesty to the set. I wanted it to be a safe, happy space for all of us. After all, if you want to see a certain colour on the canvas, you need to carry that colour on your palette too. For us, the colours were joy, care, purity, and compassion—our primary hues for the picture we were about to paint.

In hindsight, I must admit that living up to my own words was one of the greatest challenges for me. I had to see if, despite carrying the heavy burden of financial uncertainty, I could still maintain that inner sense of goodness. Of course, the core pressures of creativity as a director, writer, and actor were going to be there anyway, without any concessions. So, the question was would I be able to maintain my calmness and gentleness toward the scores of people running around me? Would I be able to walk the talk? In fact, with so many people turning their backs, this film became the only lifeline keeping me connected to the realm of goodness. I believe in treating people well, without any hidden agenda or expectations. But the realities unfolding behind the scenes were about to test me in ways I hadn't anticipated.

The work environment of any place or team is the sole responsibility of its leader. It starts at the top. So, it was my duty to ensure that the shooting atmosphere of *Tanvi the Great* mirrored the positive world we had created for Tanvi Raina. I am tempted to share some of my own interesting experiences and anecdotes, but since this was a test for me as well, I don't want my recollections to be biased. Instead, I have asked someone else to walk you through this part of the journey and let you decide for yourself whether I passed the test.

For this segment, I hand over to my colleague—my harshest critic and evaluator, the referee who watches everything with tenacious objectivity (I call it 'cold-hearted syndrome')—Herman D'Souza to recount his memoirs of the shooting days. Of course, Herman has promised to make this chapter the most objective (and I fear, driest) section of the entire book. So, without further ado, over to Herman D'Souza, CEO of Anupam Kher Studio.

> Although I have been associated with the film industry through Mr Kher for the past twenty years—having spent time on countless sets and witnessed numerous shoots—I wouldn't call myself a seasoned film producer by conventional standards. In the past, we have produced a few films like *Maine Gandhi Ko Nahin Mara* and *The Signature*, but *Tanvi the Great* was at a different level altogether. And here we were, already reeling under financial uncertainty on a film that was our biggest and most cherished production to date. To add to the challenge, our chosen location, Lansdowne, was completely unexplored and untested for film production. It was, in many ways, what India was to Columbus or, to put it more poetically, what the moon was to Neil Armstrong. The picturesque town had a large, warm heart but fewer hotels to accommodate a crew as large as ours. For most requirements, the crew had to travel

40-45 km down to Kotdwar. We were responsible for arranging three meals a day for 200-250 people over a 45-day schedule. Even something as routine as laundry became a herculean task with such a large team. And this was the very place where eighty per cent of Tanvi Raina's world was to come alive!

With just a shake of the head or a quick glance, Mr Kher and I would communicate whether the latest financial puzzle had been solved or had only become more complicated. The modest yet invaluable contributions that came in from friends in New York were a testament to the love, respect, trust, and goodwill that Mr Kher commands. But the way he carried himself and conducted his role as a leader—as the captain of a ship low on fuel—deserves its own TED Talk. It was an exceptionally challenging terrain for him, returning to direction after more than two decades, portraying one of the pivotal characters (which he often joked he hadn't had a moment to truly prepare for), and managing the production—all far removed from the familiar comforts of Mumbai studios, where most needs are just a phone call away.

He wanted to lead by example and live up to the speech he had delivered on the first day of the shoot in Mysore Colony, Mumbai. He was determined not to lose his cool or get flustered by anything. He genuinely wanted to create an atmosphere of friendly work culture and strong team spirit—the kind of workplace harmony most HR managers only dream about.

Having known him for years, I knew this wasn't an impossible task, but we had never sailed these waters before. As a creative person, you may learn to numb yourself to sudden betrayals, but as a human being navigating countless teething troubles on a shoot like this, how can it not affect you in real life? From squabbles over room allocations and the presence of prowling leopards nearby, to the logistical challenge of respectfully coordinating pickups and drops for senior artists and heads of departments—not to mention unpredictable, inclement weather—there was no shortage of reasons to feel unnerved. And yet, there was Mr Kher, calmly heading out for his morning walks with his DoP and writer, reminiscing about his childhood in Simla, which, in many ways, resembled Lansdowne today.

Of course, being the clear-sighted, goal-driven veteran that he is, Mr Kher understands both the value and the technique of staying calm. But to maintain such composure in the midst of chaos requires an exceptional kind of inner strength. I believe it was also his determination to mirror the sweet, serene on-screen world of Tanvi Raina in the real-world atmosphere on set that helped him navigate the roughest terrain and the most turbulent moments with grace. For me, it was a profound learning experience as well.

As an integral member of Anupam Kher Studio, I made it a point to interact with people, trying to gauge their mood and sentiments, What I found was that the team was genuinely very happy with the facilities and the way things were being taken care of. There were designated vehicles for each department, fixed time for meal breaks, off days between regular shoot days, and no night shifts. While the credit for all this goes to the entire team for pulling this off and not just any one individual, the truth is that none of it would have been possible had the man at the top stumbled even once.

Mr Kher and most of the heads of departments were staying at a simple state government-owned resort, Tip 'n' Top, while others were spread across private hotels in the town. Every morning, designated vehicles were ready to take everyone to the shoot location, ensuring a smooth start to each day. Mr Kher had also announced that every birthday falling within the shooting schedule should be notified to Pradyumna Rao—the designated person from Anupam Kher Studio—so that we could all come together, cut a cake, and celebrate together. It was a small gesture, but one that added warmth and a sense of community to the intense shooting schedule. This practice was kickstarted with Mr Kher's own birthday on 7 March 2024 and was religiously followed throughout the schedule. And then, of course, there was the nightly ritual of the 'word-building' game, which kicked off at exactly 8:20 p.m. around the dining table. It quickly became so popular that people and participants began looking forward to it as if it were a tournament being telecast by the local channel!

Dinner time at Tip 'n' Top became a social event in itself. Everyone staying there would gather at the long table, not just to eat, but to enjoy jokes, mimicry, storytelling, and good-natured banter—a full-course serving of laughter. On the few occasions I joined the group, I quickly realised that the word-building game had turned into a fierce competition, though Boman Irani remained the undefeated champion!

Before joining the game, Mr Kher would often be in his two-room cottage, diligently searching for the next source of funding. He would review the numbers with me, yet moments later, he would be at the dinner table, laughing and cracking jokes as if the word 'stress' didn't even exist in his vocabulary! He wasn't doing this to be a hero or protector, but to ensure that the film was made in an environment as flawless as the script intended.

By the middle of the schedule, we hit another stage where funds were running low. However, we had not compromised on the comfort of the crew. We hired one of the best catering services to make sure that everyone received the same high-quality meals—a practice not always followed in the industry. Every meal was eagerly anticipated and shared with joy by all.

As the time came for many to receive their second or third payment instalment, reminders started arriving for our accounts team. Yet, we couldn't let anyone know about the financial struggle we were facing. Not even Mr Kher's brother, Raju Kher, or his niece, Vrinda Kher, who was handling the day-to-day management of the production so efficiently, had any hint of the situation.

It was on one such day that Ankur, who sometimes accompanied Mr Kher on his early morning walks, came to me and asked, 'Why did sir say, "It is a very lonely journey," when all of us are with him?' I immediately understood the context. It was one of the rare moments when you could catch a glimpse of the inner turmoil Mr Kher was experiencing.

While we were tirelessly sending out emails, dinners were being made special by celebrity chefs showcasing their culinary skills in the kitchen at Tip 'n' Top. One night, Arvind Swamy treated us to an unforgettable array of traditional Tamilian dishes. Raju Kher delighted everyone with his famous rajma, and his wife, Reema Ji, served up authentic Kashmiri cuisine. I have a theory: good food satisfies the stomach and is soon forgotten, but great food lingers in your memory. That was certainly true for the legendary Parsi dish, akoori, prepared by Zenobia Irani. This delightful food created an atmosphere of positive energy, continually fuelling our hope.

I don't think even Mr Kher fully realised the immense impact of those dinners, the rounds of the word-building game, the video calls he made to the crew's family members, or the surprise trips to local eateries and shops in Lansdowne market (which never failed to astonish the locals) in easing the pressure on me. On day one, Mr Kher told us that a film about innocence and honesty had to be made with the utmost sincerity. So, naturally, we were all deeply concerned about every pending rupee that needed to be paid. Yet, there was our captain, not letting even a hurricane dim our smiles by even a fraction! He made sure we celebrated the journey of *Tanvi the Great* every single day.

We also celebrated at least three major festivals during the shoot—Mahashivratri, Holi, and Easter! In fact, I recently learnt that the dining hall at Tip 'n' Top, where we enjoyed our word-building games, impromptu singing, and mimicry sessions, now features a collage of our photos on the wall! The proof is in the pudding. Being the numbers person that I am, I can sum it up with a simple data point: we completed our Lansdowne schedule ten days ahead of the planned timeline! Such is the power of positivity and optimism.

One great learning for me from this experience is that if you can learn to compartmentalise your mind and avoid the spilling over of thoughts, you can do a lot more in life without becoming a sinkhole of anxiety and stress that pulls others into a similar state. Had Mr Kher allowed the financial struggles to influence his mood and demeanour, it would have not only affected the creative process but also everyone around him.

It is the job of a leader to protect the enthusiasm and motivation of each and every team member. It may not be easy, but it is also not impossible. One has to find the technique to do it, and I believe Mr Kher's method was to surround himself with people he loves and enjoys being around. So, he invited not only his mother and his brother's family to stay for a few days but also called in his childhood friends to spend time with him. Even his old roommate from NSD, actor Anand Desai, came over to become his roommate once again!

This made me realise the power of the company one keeps. If you want to be content and happy, spend your time with people who are good-hearted and joyful. It is no surprise, then, that Mr Kher has already received numerous messages from crew members urging him to start a new project simply because they want to relive the joy of being part of the Anupam Kher Studio team once again! Most of them are top-tier professionals, working with some of the mightiest production houses in the industry. Yet, they admit that the experience just doesn't compare to what they felt while working on *Tanvi the Great*. Here, I would like to reiterate that this is an entirely unbiased account from someone who observed it all from just an arm's length away. That is probably why he asked me to do something I don't even consider my strength: writing! But he yet again taught me one more life lesson: you cannot win a game that you are not enjoying.

Thank you, Herman, for your thoughtful and generous words. You have handed me quite an impressive report card!

I would like to conclude this chapter by saying that, for me, it is not just important but imperative to view life from the perspectives of others as well. And who understands that better than an actor?

First shot with Brigadier V. M. Chaudhari
(former Commandant, Garhwal Rifles)

Breathtaking bungalows of Lansdowne

It all began with them – Co-writers (Ankur and Abhishek) and Herman

Making melodies with M. M. Keeravani and his singers (Shagun and Gomathi)

Song makers – M. M. Keeravani and Kausar Munir

Costume, hair, and make-up teams with Razaa saab and Keiko

Eyes of the director – DoP Keiko

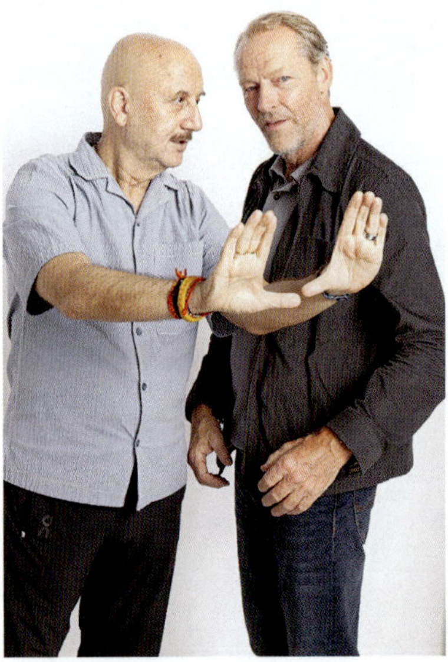

Game of direction with Iain Glen

Showtime with shogun

Who is smiling—Shubhangi or Tanvi?

Shubhangi's dance rehearsals with Kruti Mahesh

Shubhangi's fangirl moment with Iain Glen

Thinking on the edge

Silhouettes of bright minds (with Arvind Swamy)

Silence please! We are shooting.

With Razaa saab's disciples

As Colonel Pratap with the men in uniform

Haircut of cadets or an act of jealousy?

NCC cadets played Tanvi's fellow cadets at Major's Academy

Forever in love – Samar and Vidya

Day one with Pallavi Joshi and Shubhangi

Acting tough – Arvind Swamy as Major Kailash

Candid chuckles with Jackie and Boman

Even the sky looks brighter with friends

Gearing up to take off with Jackie Shroff

Table reading at Actor Prepares

Celebrating Tanvi's look with Rohit, Shipra, and Sunil

It's a wrap party!

Sharing screen and memories with Nassar

My proudest moment of all time

12

The Best Drives Are Not on Straight Roads

WHAT MANY PEOPLE MAY NOT REALISE IS THAT A FILM IS often viewed through a single lens: *'Kitna business karegi?'* (How much money will it make?) Well, that, in a way, is a dichotomy of sorts because for a true storyteller, the business of a film is not business, but entertainment and storytelling. I come from that very school of thought. Whether it is a film, a book, or any narrative form, its true purpose is to move the heart, stir the soul, and ignite the imagination. I can make this statement here, without being opposed, only because it is my book. In the world outside this book, filmmaking needs money. And so did I, as a filmmaker, even while I was playing those nightly rounds of word-building games on that rectangular table in the dining hall of Tip 'n' Top in Lansdowne!

The shoot had begun, but there was still no 'The End' to our financial quagmire. We were now almost keeping a tally of the number of people we had approached for funds. And somewhere in that counting, I stumbled upon another life lesson. It was akin to someone refusing to lend you their car because they didn't like your garage!

By God's grace, the sincerity in my work has rubbed off on my life as well. Perhaps the effort and honesty I pour into every role make people see that while I may not take myself too seriously, I am far from frivolous. Whatever I do or say comes from a place of deep and unwavering sincerity. This has earned me not only a lot of respect and recognition in my personal life but also the trust of many friends. One such friend happens to be a honcho in a leading company within a major conglomerate. This group is now closely aligned with another prominent business dynasty.

So, I met this friend and shared the outline of *Tanvi the Great*. Being a man of artistic bent and an admirer of good cinema, he expressed deep interest in the film and offered to fund it too. My mind was absorbing his words, but my heart was hearing the sound of a thousand champagne bottles popping at once! Studios had their own interpretations of my story. The royal-sized production houses had their own terms and conditions for my film. Business groups with deep pockets but shallow understanding of cinema came with their own shenanigans and complications for my production. And here was my friend—someone who commands an empire—willing to lend me a helping hand in the most honest, straightforward way, allowing me to make my film my way. God, it seemed, had been 33 per cent extra kind that day!

I don't remember which restaurant Herman booked that evening, but I do remember him ordering three or four extra glasses of wine or was it one of those imaginary champagne bottles I had heard popping in my head earlier that day?

The next morning, as my fingers typed out a heartfelt message of gratitude to my friend, my heart was hallucinating that I was playing a grand piano. He responded soon, assured me of every possible help and expressed his desire to begin the paperwork quickly.

I reached my office and headed straight to the accounts department and got it unlocked (yes, I reached that early in excitement). Stunned to see me there so early in the day, my accountant assumed that either I had joined the Income Tax department, or I was rehearsing for a sequel of *Special 26*! To his disappointment, I was still his boss, who had come to instruct him to commence the paperwork with the honcho's company. I called Herman to tell him that we must be ready with everything by the evening.

My excitement and impatience at the time might remind some of you of Seth Dharamchand from *Dil Hai Ke Manta Nahin*, where everything he did was a bit exaggerated and over the top. Dharamchand was the outrageously over-the-top father I played in the film—a role that remains one of my most memorable to date. To those outside the Mumbai film industry, it might seem unbelievable that an actor with my experience and stature was struggling to make a film he truly believed in, on his own terms. After all, how can Anupam

Kher not have producers making a beeline outside his cabin to fund his passion project? But this was the truth, and to be honest, not a bitter one for me. Simply because, while I may not empathise with all those who did not agree to back this film, I nevertheless understand their predicament. After all, each of us—including me—has had to say 'no' at some point, often to someone else's disappointment. In fact, surviving a long innings in this unpredictable industry depends more on the projects you say 'no' to than the ones you say 'yes' to. There is nothing personal about it. It is like taking punches in a boxing match; this aspect is not just part of the game, but the game itself. So, truly, no hard feelings.

With messages and emails being exchanged with the honcho himself at a swift pace, I did not have any reason to accommodate any hard feelings anyway! Soon, the honcho friend asked for some account statements and other relevant documents. With spring in his feet, Herman arranged the required details and sent them across without delay.

With an old friend at the end of the mailbox, you would think anxiety wouldn't be part of the equation. It seemed that he no longer saw our friendship in the same light as I did. Out of the blue, he adopted a very professional tone and sent a very dry, formal email, criticising our bookkeeping practices! Instead of addressing the matter of the much-needed funds, he handed out unsolicited advice on how to revolutionise our accounting systems.

Evolution is my second nature, and I am always open to constructive suggestions, especially when they come from people I value and who have greater expertise in the matter at hand. However, in this case, the intent betrayed the urgency and compassion. I hadn't approached a panel on *Shark Tank India* to pitch for seed funding. This was not about pie charts or the grammar of statistics. Of course, accounting advice was certainly welcome, and I would have happily embraced them too had they come in a spirit of collaboration. But these looked like a set of cold instructions with the intent of using them as tough-to-adhere terms and conditions for granting funds.

Time was of the essence, and there was no way we could have waited to implement all those suggestions in our accounting software first. The clock was ticking like the hackneyed time bomb that one sees in the climax of action films. The least a friend could have done in such a scenario was to show some empathy and throw me the rope I so badly needed to pull myself out of the quagmire. But the email had come without any 'attachment' (pun intended).

While my craft has taught me the importance of reading the lines carefully, life has taught me the even greater skill of reading between them. In this case, what was left unsaid spoke louder and clearer than the words themselves. I couldn't sleep well that night, clinging to the hope that the honcho would at least call to explain. But the call never came. So, I reached out to him instead! I sent a voice note to him, expressing gratitude for his generosity and consideration. I know you are expecting fireworks. Well, those were just the first two lines. What followed was a promise. I told my friend that I would make the best film of my career without borrowing a single rupee from him. I was far, far away from the destination but I declared that *Tanvi the Great* would be counted among the finest films in the world! It was not a dialogue; it was a statement of conviction and self-belief. It was also a way to convert the negative energy of rejection into the fuel for my creative fire. I believe all the rejections, denials, or betrayals can be your firewood. Just like in the gym, in life too, the tougher the workout, the stronger you get. Your conviction must ring louder than the voices of rejection and doubt. Only then can you turn a deaf ear to all the discouragement that comes your way.

The voice note may have come across as arrogant, but it was not. Confidence and arrogance are like identical twins, and the world often confuses one for the other. But as long as you can tell the difference, it doesn't matter. And I could. I knew I was going to make the best film of my career. So, we parted ways. We had to. The honcho, perhaps taken aback by my somewhat haughty response, ended the conversation. We were again on our own as far as the funds were concerned.

I must make a confession here. Not everyone may know, but there was a point in my professional life when I had lost all my money I had in the bank and, as a matter of courtesy, life introduced me to bankruptcy. It happened when I had invested large sums of my earnings into television software production (a fancy term they used back then for making TV shows and programmes) via my newly incorporated company. Our tiny boat actually sank under the weight of its own success! Several of our shows were green-lit by different satellite channels, and we suddenly found ourselves producing all of them at once. This stretched our resources thin and choked our cash flow. And before even my harshest critics could have prayed for my downfall, everything came to a grinding halt. Cash flow became a problem, and suddenly it seemed Anupam Kher had to pay half of the world! Cut to 2024, and the ghosts of those turbulent days returned to visit me every night as I lay in bed at cottage number 1, perched on the edge of the hill. Yes, I feared I might lose everything—once again.

However, we were wiser, better connected, and better prepared this time. So, we continued scouting for funds. We kept working on it in the background, even as we were shooting. Soon, we came across a company run by three or four partners based in a small city in North India. When we met them, they came across as hungry, enthusiastic, and full of ambition. They were down-to-earth, respectful, and excited enough to drive all the way to Lansdowne with their wives and kids to meet us.

They met the entire team, explored the locations, admired the outstanding work done by our art director, Urvi, praised the story once again, joined us for dinner, and shared drinks with Herman. As a producer, I knew how crucial it was to have a happy set of co-producers on board. That is why, even after a long, exhausting day of shooting, I made it a point to sit with them and make them feel comfortable.

Since they had brought us the much-needed cake of funding, it felt only fair to offer them a cherry on top. After consulting with my team of assistants, we agreed to feature one of their children in the song 'Manchalaa'—a beautiful composition by M. M. Kreem, picturised on Boman Irani. The child was enthusiastic and picked things up quickly. While his parents eventually got bored by the shooting experience—as it happens usually—they did transfer a portion of the promised funds to the account of the company we had formed as co-producers. They returned home, leaving me with a lifeline of funds and plenty of Vastu tips for my office.

Life finally seemed as smooth and straight as a newly constructed expressway. I sat back in peace, gazing at the winding road a few metres below. Its hairpin bends and serpentine curves gave it an unpredictable charm. What I didn't realise then was that the road below was about to replace the expressway in my life.

Soon enough, the flow of funds was disrupted once again. The major portion of the promised money did not arrive. We waited and then waited some more before we began to probe. That is when we discovered the truth: the partners were facing internal disagreements, and there were some accounting complications that had tangled up the entire money flow. I was not at all comfortable with this kind of money flow and the events that unfolded at their end.

This time, I didn't even have to say a word to Herman. Just one look was enough—he understood, nodded, and pulled the plug by sending them an email to cancel the association. And just like that, we were back on our own, navigating through that hairpin bend road once again.

But I realised something important: it is these very twists and turns that add beauty to our journey. A straight road downhill would not have been half as beautiful as the one we saw approaching Lansdowne. To truly appreciate the landscape of life, you have to embrace its curves. One needs to embrace and enjoy these twists and turns to appreciate the beauty of life.

13

It Is Good to Be Firm but Even Better to Be Flexible

During the shooting days, we spent most of our time filled with smiles and joy. The satisfaction of creating something special and unique, right from ground zero, was felt by everyone every single day. But one evening in April was different. Our lead actress was crying inconsolably, tears rolling down her cheeks I tried to console her, but soon realised her tears were contagious. Eyes around us turned moist, and voices grew heavy with emotion. Between the countless selfies and group photographs, a deep sense of what our lead actress identified as FOMO had possessed the entire crew. After weeks of living and working together in that small, picturesque army town, we were about to go our separate ways. That April evening marked the final time the crew of *Tanvi the Great* heard the call of 'Pack up!' in Lansdowne.

We had lived an entire lifetime out there—watching our characters come alive and a long-held dream begin to take shape. I had followed my heart more than any GPS yet arrived at the destination with remarkable precision. With 70 per cent of the film shot, we returned to the chaos of Mumbai. Though 30 per cent of the film was still left to shoot, I was now certain we had made the right choice by not giving in to market forces. And for the few miles left to be covered, we had a clear roadmap.

Shooting resumed in June. By then, it was clear that the assurances of the so-called co-producers, whom we had met in the cool surroundings of Lansdowne, had evaporated by the time Mumbai's sultry summer rolled in. Once again, finances were uncertain, but my faith in the film remained unshaken. In fact, it had grown into an indomitable belief that *Tanvi the Great* would, without a doubt, become a great film.

We shot a very important song, which is also a one-of-its-kind tribute to the valour of the Indian Army, at Yash Raj Studio. I could have shot it anywhere else, but for me, relationships are for eternity, even when the people are no longer around. *Tanvi the Great* marked a giant leap in my journey, and I wanted to do it with the blessings of Yash Ji, the legendary Yash Chopra. What he meant to me can only be understood by the fact that I specifically shot that song and a few more scenes at Yash Raj Studios, even when the finances were dwindling. Thanks to the incredibly talented, National Award-winning choreographer, Kruti Mahesh, and her wonderful team, this schedule too wrapped up pretty smoothly and on time.

Yet, in a parallel world, all the difficulties I had faced so far could easily have dulled my appetite for fresh ideas. With the financial landscape resembling the parched land we all saw in *Lagaan*, no new idea could have germinated in my mind. But ideas, I have learnt, don't wither easily—not even in drought-like conditions. They find a way to grow. And if firm decisions are the key to great outcomes, being flexible in the right proportion can become the shortcut to them. So, I opened the windows of my mind once again. This was not brash arrogance, but an unleashed hunger to deliver the best possible results as an artist and make everyone proud! And just when I had made peace with uncertainty and opened myself to possibility, creativity came calling—unexpected and unmistakable.

One afternoon, during a lunch break, not one but two brainwaves were caught by the invisible dish antenna of my mind. I remember that moment very vividly. Just like my favourite peanut chikki that accompanied every meal break, my co-writers, Ankur and Abhishek, had become a constant presence during my meal breaks. So, I immediately shared the new idea with them.

At first, they were taken aback by the idea of changing an entire character and its storyline so late in the process. They exchanged glances and communicated in their non-verbal sign language, but soon, their surprise turned into excitement. After all, who wouldn't be thrilled at the prospect of working with a Hollywood actor? Yes, that was the idea! I had decided to bring in a performer from Hollywood or international cinema. Energised by the possibility, the writing team jumped into action and started making the necessary amendments to the script.

As for Herman—whose jaw had been dropping more frequently than the stock market ever since we began this film—he surprised me this time by not being surprised. In fact, he genuinely appreciated the idea of casting an international face. I was both relieved and a little stunned. Then, after a pause, he said, 'It is a great idea . . . about as great as me buying a Ferrari.' The real question, of course, was: how do we afford it? Our budget had stretched to its limit and finally snapped, and we were really struggling. To make matters more urgent, the shoot was nearing completion, and many people were rightfully expecting the balance of their payments. And here I was, suggesting we bring in another actor from Hollywood!

The ramifications of such a move are that everyone starts assuming you are sitting on a heap of money and still acting stingy with the rest of the world. The truth is that we don't give due credit to passion when in reality, passion combined with self-belief can make you do the unthinkable. Like it made me call up my friends in Hollywood, hoping to find the right actor with enough international exposure for a very special role: a renowned autism specialist named Michael Simmons. (Yes, I came up with that name, ahead of my other two writers.)

The point to be bookmarked or highlighted here is that adversities, limitations, or obstacles can restrict you physically, logistically, or materially, but nothing should stop you from aiming for the stars. Your goals, your vision, your dreams, your aspirations—everything should remain in your control, unscathed by the events or circumstances you are in. Whenever I feel trapped by forces beyond my control, I turn to my ability to think about that small window through which light and fresh air find their way in. It is that very window that eventually becomes my escape route. So here I was—a sixty-nine-year-old actor-producer with limited financial resources, reaching out to people in Hollywood for the first film I was directing in twenty-two years. I could very well have failed to get anyone on board. But as I often say, I was so determined to succeed that I was even willing to fail for it.

Meanwhile, the character of Michael Simmons was beginning to take shape on paper. With each passing day, I could see him more clearly and that clarity made my search sharper and more focused. I had planned to keep the involvement of an international actor in *Tanvi the Great* as a surprise—our secret ace. I even made the entire crew swear an oath of silence about who they were working with. But of course, there are two kinds of people you can never keep secrets from: mothers and the media.

The day the actor landed in Mumbai, someone managed to trail him to our set and snap a photo while the two of us were deep in discussion about a scene. Within a couple of hours, my phone started buzzing with countless calls and messages from friends and colleagues, exclaiming in disbelief (some with pride, others with envy) that I had actually managed to rope in the incredibly talented actor from *Game of Thrones*, Iain Glen!

I had done it! Or so I thought, when Iain gave his approval. While *Tanvi the Great* isn't exactly a thriller, the journey of making it had its fair share of edge-of-the-seat, nail-biting moments. What could possibly go wrong now? But then, a major plot twist emerged—visa issues.

I had scheduled a table read with Iain the day before the shoot. The goal was to give him time to acclimate—not just to the Mumbai weather, but also to the crew, the co-stars, and me as the director. Invitations went out to everyone, and some crew members even flew in specifically for the table read. But it seemed the universe had a plan to truly test Iain's acting skills. His visa wasn't ready in time. To be fair to the authorities, he had been travelling on very short notice, and there was no way he could have arrived earlier. As a result, the table reading had to be cancelled, along with the special feast we had planned to introduce Iain to the Indian philosophy of *atithi devo bhava*—the belief that the guest is God.

This cancellation was unfortunate but not as scary as the thought of an international actor landing in your country, your city, for the first time, and being driven straight to your set from the airport. There was hardly any time to build any kind of rapport before calling out, 'Action!' My safety net during this time came from the many long calls Iain and I had over the previous days, where we even discussed the punctuation marks in the script with great care.

Though I am tempted to share more about Iain's stunning performance, I will refrain from turning this into a BTS (behind the scenes) chapter. All I would like to mention here is that time zones, distance, and circumstances—none of it matters if you put effort into the preparation and heart into the performance. That is exactly what Iain brought to Michael Simmons.

The change in the character—and consequently the actor—brought a new dimension to the screenplay. It took Tanvi Raina's story beyond borders. While the story was always universal at its core, with Iain's character coming in, we were able to alter the setting and deliver a message that would resonate with audiences across the globe.

There was one more unexpected improvisation I made to the end of the film. It happened during lunchtime while Ankur, Abhishek, and I were enjoying some peanut chikki. Thinking back to that moment, I realise how much I value the creative synergy I share with them—like my favourite peanut chikki and homemade meals! I won't reveal the details of this second improvisation here, though. It is something you will discover when you watch *Tanvi the Great* in theatres. It is cute, sweet, and a bit personal.

The bigger lesson I took from this experience is that it is important not to view your creation as so flawless and perfect that there is no room for improvement. It is crucial to keep the windows of your mind open. *Tanvi the Great* wouldn't have turned out as well as it did if I hadn't revisited the script after our successful main schedule in Lansdowne.

There was no self-doubt—just the belief that something better might be out there, waiting to be discovered. If you have the time and the will, there is no harm in flipping back a few pages and reassessing. The key is to look back with the intention of moving forward in an even better way—not to become indecisive. Overall, be firm, but it also pays to be flexible enough to accommodate newer thoughts and ideas.

14

It Takes an Army to Make a Film

It is neither wrong nor overconfident to say that Lansdowne will likely appear in more Google searches than ever before once *Tanvi the Great* reaches global audiences. In fact, my crew and I must have already contributed to boosting Lansdowne's search traffic since 2023! Before the film, the awareness of this army town outside of Uttarakhand was likely limited to the Delhi-NCR region, where it ranks high on the list of weekend getaways of *dilliwaalas* (people from Delhi), just after Jaipur.

Originally named Kaludanda, this small town was renamed Lansdowne in 1887 after Viceroy Henry Charles Keith Petty-Fitzmaurice, the 5th Marquess of Lansdowne (history refers to him as Lord Lansdowne). The British adopted the town as the headquarters for the Garhwal Rifles, a heroic regiment of the Indian Army. In addition to being one of India's most serene hill stations, it became home to some of the bravest men in uniform.

It is rare to come across films set against the backdrop of the army that don't focus on war or action. In other words, peacetime, non-violent army films are almost non-existent. *Tanvi the Great*, however, is an exception as it explores an aspect of the army that no other film has ever touched upon. Moreover, I grew up in Shimla (as mentioned earlier), which was once the Western Command Headquarters of the Indian Army. Because of this, I have always had a strong connection to the army, almost a deep sense of belonging. I knew that *Tanvi the Great* would be my chance to pay a heartfelt tribute to the brave men in uniform.

Naturally, many scenes were written to depict life in a cantonment town as old and charming as Lansdowne. Given the financial challenges we faced during the production, it became clear that building sets was not an option. How could we possibly recreate the authentic presence of bungalows that had stood for over a hundred years, like soulful characters in Keiko's frames?

However, seeking permission to shoot with a crew of around 250 members in Lansdowne—a town that not only serves as a cantonment area but is also the headquarters of the esteemed Garhwal Rifles—was no easy task. That said, it wasn't as difficult as it might seem. We simply had to ensure all the necessary paperwork was in order, providing detailed information about every crew member, from heads of departments down to the spot boys. I must commend the collaborative spirit of our team and the helpful attitude of the army personnel, which made the process feel smoother than it actually was.

Lansdowne is also unique from an administrative perspective, as much of the area is managed by the Army Cantonment Board. Any repairs or renovations require prior approval from the board, primarily for security reasons. We planned to shoot in several bungalows that are actually the residences of officers posted there, so our application file ended up being much thicker than the script itself!

When I first met Brigadier V. M. Choudhary, the commandant of the Garhwal Rifles, in October 2023, I was greeted with a firm handshake and a warm welcome. He shared several personal anecdotes from his time at Siachen, the world's harshest battleground. What he revealed made us realise that the bravery of these remarkable men was far beyond anything we could truly comprehend—at least a thousand times greater than what we had ever imagined.

He then introduced me to Colonel Subir Sondhi and Lt Colonel Shivam Aggarwal, who were incredibly supportive throughout the process. In them, I found my first audience in Lansdowne for the story narration. I presented the script, outlining the parts to be filmed in the cantonment area, and shared Tanvi Raina's entire journey. Their response was so encouraging that it turned the making of this film into a mission for me. It strengthened my resolve to make *Tanvi the Great* to the best of my abilities—and perhaps even beyond what I thought possible—becoming as steadfast as an officer in the Garhwal Rifles! They were enthusiastic about the story and assured me of their full support. Additionally, Nayak Anil Negi was assigned to our shooting unit for daily coordination. This dependable young man would arrive promptly at the scheduled call time, always ready to assist with whatever we needed.

As I walked out of the commandant's office and glanced around, my eyes fell on the regimental motto: *Yudhaya Krit Nishchaya* (fight with determination). Little did I know, at that moment in October, that I would soon have to embody these words. Making *Tanvi the Great* would be nothing less than a battle, demanding unwavering determination. That motto, in retrospect, felt like a message from God, preparing me for the challenges ahead.

When we arrived in Lansdowne on 1 March 2024, it was raining heavily, and the cold wave caught us off guard, as none of us were prepared for it. However, the chill was soon eased by the warmth and hospitality of the officers.

Since Tanvi Raina's grandfather was a retired Colonel, we needed to portray him living in one of the iconic old bungalows of Lansdowne. The bungalow that fit our vision was allotted to Colonel Amit Joshi. I can't find enough words to express my gratitude for his generosity in allowing us to use his home for nearly twenty days, transforming it into the residence of retired Colonel Pratap Raina—Tanvi's on-screen grandfather. Colonel Joshi's residence plays a significant role in the film, and throughout our time there, we faced no complaints—only calm, accommodating support.

Lt Colonel Aggarwal's bungalow was just a few metres away from Colonel Joshi's, where we filmed the first ten days of our Lansdowne schedule. We were looking for a nearby location to set up a makeshift dining area for the cast and department heads during lunch. It would have been a waste of time to have them travel elsewhere for meals. That is when Lt Colonel Aggarwal, with great generosity, opened the gates of his home—and his heart—and offered us the open space in his bungalow to set up the dining room.

This was no small gesture, as allowing so many people onto his property every day could have been unnecessarily bothersome. He also introduced us to his family, and we soon learnt that he was a talented painter! By offering us space in his bungalow for those ten days, Lt Colonel Aggarwal has earned a special place in my heart—one that I don't think can ever be replaced.

As Indians, even if we are fed the best cuisine every day, the urge to break the chain with the simple *ghar ka khaana* (home-cooked food) gradually possesses us for sure. Thankfully, before we could reach that state, we were graciously invited to dinners at regular intervals by the magnanimous officers.

First, we were invited by Brigadier Choudhary to the Garhwal House, the official residence of the commandant of Garhwal Rifles. While the sumptuous dinner was unforgettable in itself, the glory of that address made it all the more special. The designated residence of the commandant—over a century old—has been home to some of the most decorated officers in the regiment's history. We also discovered that Brigadier Choudhary was an exceptional storyteller with a great sense of humour.

Brigadier Choudhary's dinner was soon followed by another dinner affectionately hosted by Colonel Sondhi and his wife, Harmeet Kaur Dhindsa, who was a commanding officer at the military hospital. While they modestly referred to it as a dinner, we all agreed it was nothing short of an unforgettable feast!

Once, when we were shooting a scene with Jackie Shroff at the Garhwal mess—a location with a breathtaking view—the officers hosted a dinner for us, where their families also joined in. That night reaffirmed that there is no greater ambassador of charm than Mr Shroff. The air buzzed with excitement as countless selfies were clicked, and the evening reached its high point with an impromptu singing performance by Mr Shroff for the families of the officers.

The idea of sharing details of these anecdotes is not to make the readers envious but to give a glimpse of the joy, generosity, and warmth of our army officers. Even while they endure and overcome the harshest of conditions—whether natural or man-made—they never lose their humanity or their infectious zest for life. Their support for our film was entirely selfless. They didn't just open their homes to us, but they also made sure we left with nothing but beautiful memories.

Not just in Lansdowne, but even in Kalina, Mumbai—where we shot an important sequence—the Indian Army extended their support and made the entire process remarkably smooth for us. I remain deeply grateful to them for standing by our endeavour at every step. Our gratitude also extends to the NCC cadets, who played a meaningful role both on and off the screen. These young warriors-in-training seamlessly bridged the gap between fiction and reality. Their enthusiasm was contagious, and their presence lent a layer of authenticity to our depiction of discipline, dedication, and courage.

For some pivotal training sequences, we brought in real NCC cadets. These young cadets, already well-versed in the rigours of real-life drills, didn't just act their parts—they embodied them on screen. Repeating physically demanding takes with the same energy and discipline, their resilience was nothing short of extraordinary.

All through the shoot, even as I wrestled with financial challenges behind the scenes, I was constantly interacting with these cadets and army officers, listening to their stories of grit and bravery. In hindsight, I believe that, at some deeper level, their presence was a divine message for me to stay courageous and keep charging forward—just as they do. In their world, certainty is rare, yet they operate with absolute commitment to duty. That spirit rubbed off on me, and I kept going, refusing to get intimidated by the uncertainty on my path.

That is why, when I say it takes an army to make a film, for *Tanvi the Great*, I mean it quite literally. Thank you to the Indian Army for all the help that everyone saw as well as for the silent strength you gave me, which only I truly know.

15

Thank You, Lansdowne, for Making Us Feel at Home

I want to share something that I have not discussed with anybody else till date. While filming *Tanvi the Great*, there were several moments when I felt the urge to mention 'Lansdowne' in the scenes. So, I would improvise the lines on the spot and include its name in the dialogue. I think it was an instinctive way of expressing my gratitude to this small town with an extraordinarily large heart. I truly felt indebted to the town and its people for the warmth and generosity with which they treated us. Moreover, this town has been a quiet yet significant contributor to the world of Tanvi Raina. As I have mentioned earlier, every time I envisioned the setting of the story, I would see flashes of a small army town with a beautiful cantonment area as the abode of Tanvi's grandfather, with whom she comes to stay. And this is the reason why I felt it was my responsibility to give Lansdowne the recognition it rightfully deserves. Lansdowne deserves to be known and celebrated for its goodness and simplicity. It may sound strange or even a little irrational, but you will sense exactly what I mean when you watch the film.

I think one of the main reasons for this uncanny connection is the simplicity and purity of the place and its people. It reminded me not only of my childhood in Shimla, which was just like Lansdowne back then, but also of how the atmosphere and energy of this town naturally brought out a sense of goodness in you. The world of *Tanvi the Great* could not have been imagined or created anywhere else on this planet, and I would happily sign that off on a stamp paper! And though it wasn't the easiest place to shoot in, Lansdowne gave me some of the calmest, most grounding moments of my life—right when I needed them the most.

By now, you already know the kind of anxious baggage I arrived with. Inside, I was battling the pressure of financial uncertainty, with no real way to share what I was going through. I felt deeply alone. And yet, in that quiet town, something began to ease. The early morning walks around Tip 'n' Top, the unexpected visit to Bhulla Taal for an unforgettable *bun maska* (buttered bun) at Kaludanda Cafe, and the impromptu breakfast at Lansdowne Trip Travel Cafe—they all worked like a heavy iron smoothing out creases from a crumpled cloth. Lansdowne, in its own quiet way, became a therapy for my creative soul that was struggling to balance the commercial side of things. It was the balm I desperately needed, offering me immediate relief.

I have to share one anecdote that perfectly captures the simplicity, innocence, and honesty of the place. Often, during my morning walks, I would strike up conversations with kids on their way to school. They would get excited to see me and ask for pictures, which I was always happy to oblige. One day, I met three students—two girls and a boy—on their way to school, which was about half an hour away. We chatted for a bit about their schoolwork, favourite subjects, and so on. By this point, I had gotten used to the drill and was expecting them to ask for a picture. So, I playfully asked, *'Ab photo khinchwaani hai?'* (Do you want to take a picture now?)

The boy's frank response will remain etched in my memory forever, not just because of its simplicity, but because of the sheer honesty in it. To my surprise—and much to the amusement of Keiko and Ankur, my usual walking companions in Lansdowne—the boy said, *'Nahin, school ke liye late ho jaayenge!'* (No, we would be late for school!) This, for me, was pure *pahaadi innocence* (the innocence of people from the hills). These students, who had cheerfully greeted me, knew who I was, and had seen my movies, still kept their priorities straight. They didn't ask for a picture, and that spoke volumes about their grounded nature. I think living in the hills teaches you that nothing comes easy. One has to work hard and walk for miles even for the basic necessities. Life truly moves at a different rhythm and pace there.

I believe this simplicity is contagious. It rubs off on you and makes you appreciate life's little joys, like the French toast with coffee at this charming cafe run by a couple from

Uttar Pradesh. They left their well-paying corporate jobs in Delhi and moved to Lansdowne to live peacefully and open their own place, the Lansdowne Trip Travel Cafe. Amit and Shipra have created such a beautiful space that we ended up shooting a scene there. It wasn't in the original script, but the cafe's calming vibe and stunning view inspired us to create a scene just for that location.

Amit and Shipra have a special way of remembering all the celebrated guests who visited their cafe; they would put the guest's name on the chair they sat in. Needless to say, by the end of our shoot, every chair in the cafe had a name tag on it!

The whole crew felt the same about Lansdowne. Everyone was happy doing simple things like having samosas, chaat, or Garhwali thali at the local market. It wasn't just the cafes and food joints, the clothing and shoe shops in Lansdowne were equally welcoming. They made us feel like personal guests. Take the Javed Shoe Company, for example. Known for supplying shoes and jackets to the Indian Army, they have several shops around town. It is safe to say that during our forty-five days there, the number of shoes they sold probably surpassed their entire yearly sales! And no, it wasn't about the pricing; it was the warmth with which they would welcome us and treat us. And when I say 'us', I mean everyone, from the directors to the light-men and spot boys. It was this love that came with the items that made it all so special.

Another remarkable thing about Lansdowne is how its residents have truly embraced it as their own. Rather than relying on others for everything, they nurture the town just like a gardener tends to his garden. One such person is Dr S. P. Naithani, who has become like a foster father to the town. He and his wife graciously hosted us for an incredibly lavish dinner at their beautiful home. Life in metropolitan cities has contaminated most of us, making us forget the simple joy of visiting someone's home without any specific reason or agenda. It was so refreshing to be invited by these wonderful people, who didn't know us personally, yet wanted to share their home-cooked meal simply because we were guests in the town they call their home! Mrs Naithani is one of the most generous and affable hosts I have ever encountered.

I may not remember the names of everyone who came to meet us, helped us, or simply came to see us, but what will always stay with me is their selfless love and genuine desire to contribute to the making of our film. Whether it was the shop supplying rations to our caterer, Timmy, or the dozens of people who happily spent hours standing in the temple to be part of that beautiful bhajan we shot there, *Tanvi the Great* belongs to them as much as it belongs to me and my team.

In fact, Tip 'n' Top became a bit of a tourist spot for the entire time we were there. Word would spread about our shooting and the presence of stars like Jackie, Boman, Arvind, Pallavi, and myself at the resort. Tourists and locals from nearby towns would come in the evenings, waiting for us to return or finish dinner just to take a selfie with us. Not once did the locals do anything that made us uncomfortable.

They simply wanted that one little moment of joy, and we were happy to be part of their memories. In fact, Tip 'n' Top now has a collage of our pictures adorning the same dining hall where we spent so many evenings together.

But for me, the most special thing about Lansdowne was when my mother arrived and said, '*Yeh mera watan hai. Main yahaan pehle bhi aayi huyi hun.*' (This is my place. I have been here before.) Thank you, Lansdowne, for making my mother feel at home.

16
The Best Gifts Are the Memories We Collect

During those beautiful days in Lansdowne, along with all the love and respect we received, there were also quite a few intriguing, funny, and downright ticklish moments that kept us entertained for days. Some I experienced myself, others some were brought to my knowledge as and when they happened. I would love to share a few of them with you.

The Secret Accident of Col Pratap Raina

This one turned out to be unintentionally funny. We had been invited to Dr Naithani's residence for dinner. A few members of the team had arrived early and were waiting for me when they noticed a bit of a commotion down the road. They saw that a four-wheeler had toppled over into a dry drain, and people were trying to pull it out. A closer look revealed that it was our vehicle! It was the same Maruti Suzuki Gypsy that my character, Col Pratap Raina, drives in the film.

Now, I can only go by the official version I was told: apparently, some animal suddenly leapt in front of the vehicle, and in order to avoid hitting it, the driver swerved a bit too sharply. In doing so, he lost control, and the Gypsy tumbled down the cliff. Thankfully, the driver jumped out just in time and escaped with minor bruises. But the car was in pretty bad shape.

My production team, trying to manage the situation on their own, decided not to inform me about the accident right away because they didn't want to worry me late at night. So, they decided to tow the vehicle discreetly through a shortcut suggested by some helpful locals. Now here is where it turned into a full-blown comedy of errors. The suggested 'shortcut' turned out to be the very road in front of Dr Naithani's house! And just as my car pulled up and came to a halt outside his gate, the mangled Gypsy showed up too—right on cue. I stepped out of the car and was greeted by some very familiar but very nervous faces, as if their haemoglobin levels had dropped on the spot.

They had tried so hard to keep the incident under wraps, but sometimes God breaks news faster than any reporter. They stood there speechless, while I, of course, was only concerned about the driver's safety. Thankfully, he was fine. With that relief, we were able to enjoy the wonderful dinner hosted by the Naithanis, who made us feel truly at home with their affection and hospitality.

The Mysterious Choir

By the time Good Friday rolled around, we had started shooting gruelling outdoor sessions. The sun seemed to be in a rush to bring in summer, and the days were starting to feel a bit more draining. This particular incident happened in the wee hours of Easter morning. After a physically exhausting shoot and some late-night planning with my associates for the next day, I had finally dozed off in my cottage at Tip 'n' Top. My assistant, Dattu, was in the room next door.

Sometime between 3 and 4 a.m., while it was still pitch dark outside, the sound of a church choir filled my room. I sat up in bed, startled. It honestly felt like a huge choir was performing inside my cottage with the kind of deep, resonant reverberations you would hear in a cathedral. It took me a moment to figure out that the divine harmonies weren't coming from some hidden choir tucked away in the closet or bathroom, but they were blasting from my Bluetooth speaker!

I breathed a sigh of relief only for my left brain to immediately kick in with a very valid question: Who on earth played this choir through your Bluetooth speaker in the middle of the night? Even if it was accidental, there was no one else around, and no device anywhere near enough to connect to it. And I certainly hadn't sleepwalked my way into opening a music app or a YouTube channel and picked a church choir of all things! So how was it playing?

I scrambled to switch it off, but all the tiny colourful lights of the speaker were blinking at once. It was a sight I had never seen before, and honestly, one I will never forget. I took the speaker outside, and by then, Dattu had woken up too. He looked at me, totally confused, wondering why I was suddenly so enthusiastic about celebrating Easter! Somehow, he managed to shut it off. But my eyes? Yeah, they were in no mood to shut down after that.

All the mysterious stories I had ever heard or read about Lansdowne started flashing through my mind. My single-screen theatre of a brain—till then showing nothing but *Tanvi the Great* on loop—suddenly turned into a full-blown multiplex running a horror film festival! I don't think I have ever longed for daybreak with as much earnestness and intensity as I did on that Easter morning.

I shared this incident with everyone I met that day, but no one could explain why that choir played in my room of all things, on Easter morning! The case remains unsolved to this day. And honestly, I am too scared to even try getting to the bottom of it.

Tigers and Their Dad

From the day we landed in Lansdowne, the locals and the staff at Tip 'n' Top had been telling us how common leopard sightings were in the area. Apparently, leopards could be seen casually crossing roads, resting near the church crossing, strolling along pavements, and snatching up small animals (quick snacks for them) right out of people's backyards. Honestly, I wouldn't have been surprised if someone claimed to have spotted a leopard sipping chai and munching on rusk at a roadside kiosk.

Amit and Shipra, the lovely folks who run that picture-perfect cafe, often invited the crew to join them on leopard-spotting drives after the sunset. I am still not sure whether it was me or the leopard people were more scared of but not a single person ever accepted their invitation.

The leopard, however, didn't need an invitation nor was it the least bit intimidated by me. So, it decided to meet and greet the crew on its own terms. Quite a few crew members claimed to have spotted it prowling near their hotels. Thankfully, none of them felt the urge to take a selfie with the beast—though they did take plenty with the best!

Leopard sightings were something even the Army officers had alerted us about. But were we prepared for a tiger? (Well, a tigress, to be precise.) That unexpected twist happened when Jackie Shroff was with us for his shoot. He was staying with us at Tip 'n' Top. That night, some of our crew members heard growls and grunts outside. Soon, those sounds turned into what could only be described as a mild roar. In fact, a couple of them even felt like someone—or something—was trying to push their doors open. This was Tip 'n' Top, remember.

By morning, the town was buzzing. Locals were talking about spotting a tigress and her cubs nearby! Later that day, a few crew members confirmed they had actually seen her, walking down the road with two or three cubs. The news and the visual image of that majestic tigress strolling by kept all of us hooked for days.

I mentioned this episode to Jackie as well and told him to be a little more careful, as he had this habit of wandering around the resort after dinner. He turned around, looked at me, and said, 'Don't forget, I am tiger's daddy!' Even my writers couldn't have come up with a better comeback to that one!

These countless memories are Lansdowne's true souvenirs, etched not on paper or postcards, but in the soul . . . just like *Tanvi the Great*.

There are so many stories, so many moments from those days that will stay with me forever. It still amazes me that a film that almost didn't happen ended up changing so changing us. The making of this film quietly recharged our goodness circuits. It made us a little calmer, a little lighter, a little more tuned in to the simple joys of life. Moreover, it has given me precious life lessons many of which I have shared with you through these pages. And I promise you this: you will enjoy watching *Tanvi the Great* even more than you enjoyed reading about it.

Jai Ho.

17
In Their Own Words

When I began this beautiful journey, I had no idea who would come along to help bring this world to life. But as I moved ahead, one step at a time, the team began to take shape, and by the time we reached the table read, I was surrounded by the most amazing, sincere professionals from across the filmmaking spectrum.

There was no master plan, no big checklist, no pre-decided preferences when it came to picking my team. I met people with an open mind. The only real filter I had—beyond their talent, of course—was that they needed to be good human beings. People who were kind, compassionate, and respectful of the sensitive subject matter of the film. I also knew that we were going to spend a lot of time together, and it was important for me that we genuinely enjoyed each other's company.

I truly believe God was in a generous mood because what I ended up with was the perfect team—brilliant minds with beautiful hearts. And yes, I will say without hesitation that this was the best team in the world to build the world of *Tanvi the Great*.

As I have already shared, *Tanvi the Great* wasn't just a story for me—it became a bridge to the goodness within me. It renewed my faith in innocence, simplicity, selflessness, and love. But I was also curious to know what *Tanvi the Great* meant to my team. Was it just another professional assignment? Or did it become something more? Did it simply add another credit to the resume, or did it leave a deeper imprint? And perhaps most importantly, I wondered if the pressures I was carrying inadvertently spilt over and impacted the work environment.

So, let's hear from the people who walked this journey with me and discover what *Tanvi the Great* meant to them.

Rohit Chaturvedi – Serendipity of a Fanboy

As filmy as it may sound, it all started with a call from Mr Anupam Kher, saying he was starting a film, directing it, and wanted to meet me for the same. Little does he know that I have forever been a fan of his work—*Saaransh* and *Lamhe* have been my favourite films since childhood—and even after spending over twenty years in the film industry, I still feel a flutter in my heart whenever a childhood idol reaches out to collaborate with me.

Cut to: I am sitting in the waiting area of his office, moments away from my first in-person meeting with Mr Kher. This waiting room (one has to see it to believe it) is a lesson in humility for the world. It is filled with at least

200 trophies, awards, and accolades, and these amazing letters of love and appreciation from all over the world. Sitting in that room is one of the most inspiring experiences I have ever had. It leaves an indelible mark on you.

Soon, I was called into the private office, and from the word go, I was made to feel so comfortable and welcomed. I was simply floored—not just by the truckloads of charm, but by the warmth and appreciation the man has for film technicians, and the sheer love and passion he holds for what we aspire to create cinematically.

Moreover, one can try, but it is almost impossible not to give in to his continuous onslaught of wit and love, which doesn't spare anyone. Right from the word go, the alacrity and enthusiasm with which he narrated *Tanvi the Great* to me—the childlike eagerness to tell a story so personal to him in the most endearing way—left little choice but to fall in love with Tanvi and the beautiful musical world he wanted to create.

Clarity of thought and vision is what we technicians crave to create a cohesive world that a director envisions. It is often a challenge to bring so many creative visions together and make it all feel so effortless. In my twenty years of working as a costume designer, Tanvi has been one of the most challenging characters to create. The very clear brief from sir (I lovingly call Mr Kher that) was that he didn't want any of the characters reduced to exaggerated caricatures, nor did he want a dull, hyper-real-looking film.

I had to do a lot of research on autism to understand and create Tanvi and the world around her. I have also humbly tried to create a very unique yet real-looking world for the film. It is very challenging to design looks for characters who are not from the everyday world we observe around us. There is a fine balance between being cinematic and being respectful toward the character one is building—a balance sir wanted all of us to be especially cognizant of. With sir, the process became a lot more enjoyable and productive because, from the very start, he created an inviting and collaborative environment where we could thrive and bring our best to the table.

Another thing worth noting was that rarely do you get a set devoid of agenda and politics and *Tanvi the Great* was one of those rare exceptions. Sir had created an environment where everyone felt valued and welcomed, your presence was appreciated, and your opinions were heard, thoughtfully debated, and often embraced. All the creative freedom and the safe space he fostered for cinematic expression encouraged us to give our best to *Tanvi the Great*—our small little film with the biggest heart ever!

Working on *Tanvi the Great* has been one of the most creatively and personally enriching experiences of my life. Much of the credit goes to our director, producer, and collaborator, Mr Anupam Kher. His generosity and vision made it possible for us to work so seamlessly with such exceptionally talented technicians and artists. I hope we get to experience many more such fulfilling collaborations like *Tanvi the Great*!

Urvi Ashar – A Mother's Perspective

They say space is the most valued form of luxury in the city of Mumbai and who would know that better than an art director? But there is something even rarer in the city: calmness. In Lansdowne, I found both of these luxuries in abundance. The town was visually breathtaking and remarkably serene, and the locations I worked at mirrored these qualities. Anyone who has been on an under-construction film set knows how chaotic things can get. But in Lansdowne, every member of my team was calm and focused and genuinely enjoyed the work.

Anupam sir's vision was very clear about the visual flavour for this film. He wanted to evoke the classic old-world charm of an army town founded in the colonial era. A place that was almost untouched or uncontaminated by time. This was supposed to be most evident in 'Basera', the house of Colonel Pratap Raina, the protagonist's grandfather. Similarly, the bungalow that was supposed to be musician Razaa Saab's house had to look like a quasi-museum of music. The best part was that we actually got to work in bungalows that dated back to the early 1900s! So, the architecture of these properties itself buttressed and augmented our efforts and amplified the impact of our work manifold.

Anupam sir was one of the coolest bosses a team can wish for. He told me once that he expected the shooting location to kindle the right vibes for the actors. I think that was the objective behind shooting most of the film on real locations. The work environment was also very enjoyable and fair throughout. We requested Anupam sir to visit the set only after we had completed our work, and he graciously agreed without hesitation. He really didn't have to, but he was kind enough to do that. It reflects the amount of faith he puts in his team. There were many women on my team, and he would often quip, 'Girl power is so strong, it can even kick the director off his own set!'

I am grateful to Anupam sir for being such a supportive and open-minded boss. He gave me the creative freedom to express both the art and the emotional depth of the characters through my sets. His trust in us created a completely stress-free environment for me and my team. This is also the reason why I felt comfortable enough to invite my daughter to Lansdowne to stay with me for a few days.

The joy I brought home from working on this film wasn't just about creative satisfaction or ergonomics. Somewhere, as a mother of a teenage daughter, I had also connected with the storyline. It was relevant, contemporary, and deeply relatable. Although it didn't happen consciously, my mind had put me in the shoes of Vidya (Tanvi Raina's mother). I got drawn towards the mother-daughter relationship. It taught me that sometimes not everyone will agree with your decisions as a parent and that all kinds of opinions will be thrown at you. But if you truly believe your decision is the right thing to do for your child, then don't bother about what others have to say. It wouldn't be incorrect to say that *Tanvi the Great* did make me a stronger mother! I understood and empathised with the soul of this beautiful film quite clearly, and because of that, I was able to push my abilities to do a little more than what I thought was my best.

To sum up my experience, I would say that a film has a lot to do with what we shoot and what is going on with us while we are shooting it. And usually, you can feel the magic in the air while filming something special, and all of us felt that while working on *Tanvi the Great*. This film is truly special, and it will always hold a lasting place in my heart.

Keiko Nakahara – One for My Son

You already know the see-saw of 'yes' and 'no' I had to cross before joining the wonderful team behind *Tanvi the Great*. While AK sir was returning to direction after twenty-two years, I was stepping into motherhood for the very first time. We both had to give our best, and so we got busy with our lives after that brief interaction. The dates, the commercial aspects, the preparation time needed, my stay in India—everything required a lot of thinking and planning. I found it easier to say 'no' than to go through all of that.

Then came the day that changed everything. I took my son to a doctor in Japan because he wasn't responding to us the way a toddler of his age typically would. That is when the doctor told me that my son was autistic. Shaken by the diagnosis and unsure how I would handle it as a single parent, I returned home, overwhelmed. That is when my sister told me AK sir had called from India. When I called him back, he told me about this film and its subject. The moment I heard about the film, a voice in my head said, 'You need to do this.' I felt that through its making, I might learn more about autism. In other words, more than the money or the chance to work with AK sir, it was the opportunity to undergo a crash course of sorts to become a more equipped, more understanding mother.

Of course, I am glad that I made that decision—not just because of the crash course angle, but because it was actually creatively very stimulating to be the director of photography for *Tanvi the Great*.

Time, however, wasn't on my side. I lost valuable days and had very little room for prep. The first sequence we shot was of Tanvi and her mother, Vidya. That was a warm-up because the real journey began in Lansdowne, where we arrived just a week before the shoot started. So, I didn't have elaborate recce sessions. Everything and everyone was new to me except Palash.

One of the biggest blessings was the natural beauty of Lansdowne and the distinctive architectural character of the places where we were shooting. Beautiful locations and great actors make any cinematographer's job easier, and I was fortunate to have both. That said, the first couple of weeks weren't easy, to say the least. AK sir is not a technique- or textbook-driven director. In fact, he is anything but conventional. There is a lot of spontaneity in his approach and visualisation. One has to stay on high alert at all times for on-the-spot improvisations. But with time, we began to understand each other better and found a natural rhythm.

AK sir's enthusiastic exclamations—'Keiko! You are the best!'—after almost every frame or shot became booster shots of encouragement for me. Soon, that phrase turned into our own special way of greeting each other. I also started responding with a heartfelt, 'You are the best!' every time he called me the best.

Every evening at the dinner table, he would very sweetly pour me a drink. My seat was fixed—the one right next to him on that long table—so he could easily ensure I was trying the best dishes being served. He appreciated my love for Indian food, and when we were in Mumbai, he treated me to the finest Japanese cuisine. In fact, all our schedule wrap dinners were held at Japanese restaurants. He would also often ask about my son and even made several video calls to speak with him and my sister in Japan. Whenever a new actor joined the shoot, he would spend a little extra energy praising me and my work. These small, affable gestures of warmth made me feel valued and absolutely comfortable.

I hope to work with more directors and producers who, like AK sir, truly recognise the value of thoughtful gestures and sincere effort. These things may seem small, but they are what build great chemistry on set. Filmmaking is a team sport, after all, and you need trust and understanding with everyone for the best results.

Leading a team of diverse people and age groups while making every single soul feel important is an art I learnt from AK sir. He understands that working together isn't just about dealing with people; it is about dealing with emotions . . . sensitive, vulnerable, fragile emotions. Not even once did he raise his voice at anyone. His calmness on set was like a light diffuser, softening the harsh glare. He always gave me enough time to be fully satisfied with the lighting and never pressurised me to hasten the process. In fact, on a few occasions, when we were shooting outdoors, I suggested an early pack-up due to the diminishing quality of light. He readily understood my point and agreed. That is not something you can expect from many filmmakers.

I came to realise that AK sir has this remarkable intuitive ability to embellish a scene because he is so focused. He kept thinking about the scenes, the performances, and the audience's emotional journey, even when we went on our morning walks and while enjoying French toast at a cafe! All this made me realise that this was not just another film being made. It was a dream, a commitment—woven together, thread by thread—with a lot of respect and love. I think I was destined to become the cinematic eyes of AK sir.

Did it all eventually make me a better mother? Well, that is something only my son can answer when he grows up. But yes, seeing Tanvi come alive through my lens, all I can say is that I am extremely proud of my son. When I went back to Japan after our Lansdowne schedule and lifted him in my arms, I felt I understood his blabber and gazes much better. I knew I had no reason to worry about him.

I have travelled across the globe and worked with some of the best talents in the world of cinema. I have done all kinds of films in India as well. That is why I mean it when I say this to you, AK sir, 'You are the best!'

Abhishek Dixit and Ankur Suman – Building a Dream, Twig by Twig

Anupam sir was shooting for *Vijay 69* when we were locking in the first draft of the film. Our meetings used to take place either at his office or at his residence.

One day, as we walked into his living room, we saw him sitting with a huge grey-coloured sling around his shoulder. He had fallen and fractured his shoulder while shooting a cycling sequence. That is when we learnt he was doing a film about a man participating in a triathlon at the age of sixty-nine! He told us that at sixty-eight, he had taken up cycling, swimming, and most importantly, embarked on the journey of making a film called *Tanvi the Great*.

Although Anupam Sir had spoken to both of us separately—around late December 2022—about his niece Tanvi and his desire to make a film inspired by someone like her, it wasn't until March 2023 that he officially brought us together as a team. We were complete strangers at the time, with only three things in common: a connection to Lucknow, a background in advertising, and names that happened to start with the same letter.

Anupam sir could see the potential of this group. He was confident he had found the right 'Jai' and 'Veeru'. By the time we reached Lansdowne, people would often ask us, *'Aap donon kitne saal se saath mein likh rahe hain?'* (How long have you two been writing together?) While we can claim our share of credit for the camaraderie we built, a big part of it goes to Anupam sir. He created a writing environment where neither of us ever felt more or less important than the other—a truly balanced collaboration.

Both of us previously worked on films, teaming up with people like Sooraj Barjatya and the late Satish Kaushik—people whose love for cinema is unparalleled. But *Tanvi the Great* was something else entirely—an experience that is hard to put into words (though, as writers, we cannot get away with that shortcoming!) It truly felt as if Anupam sir had been chosen by the universe to tell this story. Here is just one example: Anupam Sir once told us about recurring flashes he saw in his dreams of an intense and uncanny event where an old man was trying to save his little granddaughter with a doll. Dreams may not always reflect reality, but sometimes, reality carries the weight of a dream. This dream, in a way, helped us shape the relationship between Tanvi Raina and her grandfather, Pratap. It also offered us a way to explore the fate of Tanvi's father. And in the film, the grown-up Tanvi carries a doll named Cheenu—the same one she left behind at Pratap's house years ago.

As the writing progressed and the emotional anatomy of the principal characters started taking definitive contours, discussions on casting began. While it may seem implausible to many, Anupam sir was actually his own last choice for the role of the grandfather. His initial plan was to focus solely on directing the film.

Step by step, our emotional investment in the film deepened. His dream, his passion, the emotion in his eyes, and the tremble in his voice—all of it left a profound impact on us. We understood, without a doubt, what this film meant to him. Each day, we added new branches and leaves to the story, and before we knew it, we had grown a tree of life.

We watched as Anupam sir began assembling his team. In fact, we were present when he made his very first call to M. M. Kreem sir for the music. He stepped out to speak to the legendary composer and returned about fifteen minutes later with the thrilling news that we now had an Oscar winner on board! From there on, almost every meeting brought news of another impressive name joining one department or another. Anupam Sir kept us informed about every new development, treating us as true creative partners.

Beyond updates on the evolving crew, he regularly shared updates from his meetings with industry colleagues and financiers. We are genuinely grateful to him for including us at every step of the journey. Moreover, our involvement didn't end with submitting the final draft; he continued to give us an active role in the film's making, offering invaluable exposure and learning opportunities along the way. In fact, we became his designated meal companions while working on this film. We had every meal of the day with him. What started as a schedule-induced activity transformed into a cherished ritual.

To ensure our writing was technically accurate, he even arranged meetings for us with highly decorated ex-servicemen and autism experts. Despite everything on his plate, he continued to push himself—sleeping less and staying committed to his physical fitness. What stood out most was that, unlike many other production houses, he was doing almost everything himself with steady support from Herman, of course. He didn't rely on any paraphernalia to make things happen. Instead, he rolled up his sleeves and got directly involved. It was, we believe, the power of his aura and determination that made shooting in Lansdowne possible.

It would not be an exaggeration to say that his energy levels and passion proved to all of us that age is just a number. We marvelled at his ability to blend with people of all age groups. He was truly like a bird building its nest—twig by twig. And there was no commercial ambition or agenda behind all these efforts. The only motivation was to share the story of an innocent soul and the purity of heart with the world because we all know that we need such stories to reinstate our faith in the power of goodness. And he did all this at an age when most people think of taking it easy and resting on their past laurels. We learnt from him how to love life and keep growing with the hunger of a newcomer and the maturity of a seasoned mind. The truth is that working on this film has enriched us in more ways than one. It taught us how a story can be more than just a form of entertainment—it can be a deeply soulful experience.

When a character like Tanvi is brought to life, you can't help but start believing in her goodness and slowly, it begins to influence your own behaviour. You start seeing the world differently. Instead of reacting impulsively to people's actions, you pause and reflect on why they might behave the way they do. One of the most profound lessons we took from *Tanvi the Great* was that it is not just autistic children who are special; their families and friends are equally remarkable. Our respect for these families has grown immensely. There was a dialogue in the script that didn't make it into the final cut, but it captured this idea beautifully. One character corrects another by saying, 'She is autistic, not artistic,' to which the other character responds, 'She is artistic. The world just didn't get the spelling right.'

Every scene of the film brought new insights and life lessons and as writers, we evolved with each one. This journey was more than just making a film; it was about something far deeper and transformation. It completely changed our perspectives on relationships, aspirations, and dreams for the better. Thank you, sir!

Aditya Shastri – A New Dimension Added to the 5th Dimension

For us at 5th Dimension (that is the name of my company that undertakes line production), working as line producers on *Tanvi the Great* was like stepping onto a roller coaster without having the faintest clue where the tracks were going or if there were even tracks to begin with. All we knew was that this was no ordinary film. It was a whirlwind of passion, offering a kind of learning you can't find in any manual.

Anupam sir, as we affectionately call him, brought an energy to the sets that was infectious. I remember him saying, 'Films are made with passion, not with budgets and spreadsheets.' We nodded vigorously, partly because it was profound and partly because we had no choice but to make it work without spreadsheets. This wasn't just filmmaking; it was an adrenaline-fueled leap into the unknown.

Anupam sir wasn't just a director; he was a force of nature. Watching him work was like attending a masterclass in filmmaking every single day. He wasn't about rushing through scenes or settling for mediocrity. He would take his time, coaxing out performances, nurturing the smallest details, and ensuring that every frame was steeped in passion. In other words, it wasn't just about saying, 'Cut, next.' It was about asking, 'Did we feel that? Did it move us?' That level of dedication was humbling and slightly terrifying when you realised you had to keep up with it.

I remember one particularly freezing night in Lansdowne. A call came at midnight from Anupam Sir about the rooming list needing urgent attention. I was half-asleep when I realised some of the crew had a problem with their rooms, and Anupam sir went in to resolve it. When I muttered something about how making a film isn't a 100-meter sprint but a marathon, Anupam sir paused and laughed. 'Good,' he said, then added, 'I hope you are ready for the next leg.'

It was such a classic moment—him taking our madness in stride while keeping the ship sailing smoothly.

Lansdowne itself was a mix of heaven and havoc. The beauty of the place was unmatched, but managing a shoot in those conditions wasn't for the faint-hearted. Watching Anupam sir, we realised what it means to be a part of a film where passion drives every frame and how that energy spills over into the crew, the cast, and the story itself. And let's talk about those performances. The lead actress was magical in her portrayal of Tanvi Raina. There were moments we would watch her on set and feel like she was no longer acting. As for the rest—Anupam sir himself, Jackie Shroff, Boman Irani, Arvind Swamy, Pallavi Joshi, and Iain Glenn—they weren't just actors in this film. They were dreamers, storytellers, and co-conspirators in this mad, wonderful journey. And Keiko Nakahara, our director of photography? Let's just say her camera was her weapon, and she wielded it with the precision of a samurai.

It is funny now, but at the time, the lack of sleep, the never-ending surprises, and the logistical puzzles felt insurmountable. Yet, we learnt something profound: films like this aren't made with perfect plans. They are made with heart, grit, and a belief that what you are doing matters. At its core, *Tanvi the Great* was about breaking moulds and embracing the unknown. It was about capturing something real, something extraordinary, and putting it on screen.

When the film wrapped, we were exhausted but transformed. We didn't just grow as professionals—we grew as people. I wouldn't trade the experience for anything. *Tanvi the Great* wasn't just a film. It was a marathon we didn't know we were ready for, but somehow, we crossed the finish line, and it was beautiful! Also, just to clarify, yes, we survived, and yes, we would do it all over again. Tanvi, the character, lives on in all of us now.

Joshua Upputuru – The Man Who Faces the After-Effects, Literally

I know it is hard to come up with a headline that can draw your attention more than the phonetics of my surname. But then, that is the best way to introduce myself as far as *Tanvi the Great* is concerned. For a smoother narrative, I am compelled to share—strictly on a 'need-to-know' basis—that I am fortunate enough to be a member of the great Kher family. Yes, you deduced it right! I am married to Tanvi Anand's *mausi* (maternal aunt), Bhavna.

My first and formal introduction to *Tanvi the Great* happened when Anupam sir (of course, that is not what we call him when we meet personally, but since this is 100 per cent about my professional association on this film, I must address him the way I do when we are at work) played the most special and sweet *bhajan* (devotional song) from the film at home. He had come back with a heart full of melodies from M. M. Kreem's studio in Hyderabad. The moment he played it on his new toy—the Bose speaker that we all have named Kamandal—we all knew he was making something very, very special and straight from the heart.

We discussed the progress on the prep work going on for the production and how he planned to shoot the songs, capturing the imaginative mind of Tanvi Raina. He shared the idea of depicting Tanvi's happiness through an imaginary bird throughout the film. Having spent years in advertising, production, and uber-cool studios specialising in advanced VFX-based shoots, I became even more curious about the film. I felt this sudden but sincere urge in my gut—or perhaps in my heart—to be a part of this film that promised to redefine the concept of storytelling in Indian cinema. But there was no vacant berth available by then. I was so eager that I was ready to board even without a ticket!

It was Pranit who told me about the possibility of an RAC berth! He suggested that with my experience in line production, it could help if I joined the team but only if Anupam sir allowed, of course. We spoke to Mr Shastri, who, in a lighter vein, quipped whether I intended to supervise them. While I was still making up my mind whether to smile sheepishly at his comment or laugh out loud, it was decided that I would take charge of post-production supervision. I had no reason to let go of this great opportunity to be a part of *Tanvi the Great*; designation or role did not matter much. This was January 2024, and the shoot was about to commence in February!

Joining late is akin to joining a new school in the middle of the academic session. Not only is the syllabus half-done by then, but you also find it difficult to penetrate the pre-formed circles of friends. The same thing happened to me.

Although it was not a school and the people around me were really nice and warm, no one had the time to spare and explain things to me elaborately. I had to catch up on my own.

Initially, it was not very easy to make people understand my point of view or the reason behind my suggestions. I cannot blame them, though, because a lot of it was related to the post-production stages, the after-effects, and the VFX. Therefore, no one could visualise the requirements as accurately as I could. On top of that—and this was purely my personal thought process—being related to Anupam sir also meant that I had to be doubly thoughtful in my interactions with the people around me. After all, I did not want anyone to feel that I was stepping on their toes just because I had the advantage (though it wasn't really an advantage) of access to the captain of the ship.

It took me some time and several rounds of coffee to build rapport and make friends. I used to report on time, find a suitable spot next to the monitor, observe, and suggest matters within my scope of work. But this was not like a typical film shoot unit. Anupam sir personally took care of everyone and was there for all of us. The work environment was incredibly friendly and warm. No wonder, I must say, some of the friends I made on the shoot are friends for life now!

Things started making sense gradually. I was more in control of my department. Sir also developed a decent level of faith in me as a professional, and of course, the film was shaping up beautifully. To give you some context of my scope of work, I must share—without revealing much—that *Tanvi the Great* has about forty-five minutes of heavy-duty VFX with great detailing. It can easily win the distinction of being the first non-action and non-fantasy Indian film with that much VFX.

I selected a team of enthusiastic professionals, whom I knew through some previous professional collaborations, to partner with me on the VFX. The duo had shown impressive capabilities and had their fundamentals of physics in place. If it is true that God lives in detail, then I cross-checked His address almost obsessively, frame by frame.

We had commenced the basic groundwork at the shoot itself, but the real work started happening as soon as we left Lansdowne. There was a humongous volume of data to work on. Since the chosen team was based out of Hyderabad, my work base shifted there as well.

We had a full building with about eighty people working in dark rooms, day in and day out, on this film. There was a lot of work, and some really smart professionals armed with new-age techniques and technologies were creating the world of *Tanvi the Great* on their screens. Days melted away into weeks, and weeks solidified into months. In between, Anupam sir also visited the studio whenever he was in Hyderabad for music.

In the interest of honesty, I must mention that the time spent on the VFX did exceed the timeline estimates that were agreed upon initially. This also happened because we had been extremely sensitive to the quality of the output.

The results had to be world-class. That is why we added more teams to the process in Mumbai. I must also add here that Ishaan and Pranit supported me at every step in producing results that would soon be proudly shown to the world at film festivals of global reputation. Yes, all of this did test my limits professionally, physically, and personally, but it also made me stronger like never before. And five months, some five hundred cups of black coffee, and over a hundred sleepless nights later, I am proud to be a contributor to the world of Tanvi.

I would like to conclude by saying that in real life, there is no provision for VFX to fix our mistakes. Therefore, no amount of advancement in technology can ever replace the sincerity of our intent and commitment. If you have these with you, mountains can move or even be created!

Epilogue

When I first set out to make *Tanvi the Great*, I believed I was telling a story. But somewhere along the way, I realised that the story was telling me. It was teaching me about innocence, about strength, and about believing in yourself.

On this journey, there were challenges—many of them. Moments of doubt, of exhaustion, of wondering whether we were asking for too much from a dream. But every twist, every delay, every unexpected turn only made the journey richer. Because real magic is never planned. It is discovered when you stay open, when you trust, and when you keep going.

If this book has given you a glimpse into a journey that, despite all its trials and tribulations, was worth every step, if it has shown you the power of pursuing a belief with everything you have, if it has offered you not just insight into what it took to make *Tanvi the Great*, but also a few valuable lessons about life itself, then I believe it has done its job.

This may be the end of the book, but it is only the beginning of Tanvi's extraordinary story—one the world can identify with. Now that you know how she came to life, we hope you will find it both interesting and inspirational to meet her on screen.

Acknowledgements

Heartfelt gratitude to all those who promised to fund our film but never followed through. It was your broken promises that pushed me to the wall—the spot where I have always fought my best battles. Your absence lit a fire that made me dig deep and put in the kind of effort that ended up becoming a book.

A special thanks to Ankur Suman, my co-writer on *Tanvi the Great*, for helping me piece together all the memories and for being that rare, patient listener every storyteller hopes to find.

'The gateways to wisdom and knowledge are always open.'

Louise Hay